# Threads of Resilience

## Weaving a Life Worth Living

By

Stephen Watathi



**KDP ISBN:** 9798397275057
**Imprint:** Independently published

# Table of Contents

# Introduction

In the heart-wrenching and captivating pages of "*Threads of Resilience: Weaving a Life Worth Living,*" we are drawn into a world where the extraordinary intertwines with the ordinary, and the human spirit shines amidst the shadows. With prose that paints vivid pictures and dialogue that crackles with emotion, we embark on an unforgettable journey alongside Emily Williams—a woman whose life dances between triumph and tragedy, resilience and vulnerability.

As the story unfolds, we are granted intimate access to the tapestry of Emily's life, meticulously woven with threads of hope, heartache, and the tenacity to rise from the ashes. With each turn of the page, we are transported to the depths of her darkest moments, where the weight of her struggles threatens to consume her. We feel the chill of despair as she battles her inner demons, her heartache echoing through the silent nights.

But within the darkness, a flicker of light emerges—a testament to the indomitable human spirit. With each triumph, we witness Emily's resilience shining brightly, like a beacon in a storm. We stand beside her as she dusts herself off after each fall, her determination unwavering, her spirit unyielding.

The pages come alive with the sights, sounds, and emotions that permeate Emily's journey. Cinematic descriptions transport us to the bustling city streets, where the cacophony of life surrounds her, mirroring the tumult within her own heart. The scent of exotic spices fills our nostrils as we accompany her on her travels, immersing ourselves in vibrant marketplaces and serene temples. The air crackles with anticipation as she confronts her deepest fears, and we hold our breath, rooting for her every step of the way.

Embedded within the narrative are poignant dialogues that stir our souls and resonate with our own experiences. We hear the raw vulnerability in Emily's voice as she confides in her allies, sharing the triumphs and tribulations of her journey. Words of wisdom from mentors and fellow seekers of truth linger in our minds, as we internalize the powerful life lessons they impart.

As we turn the final page of this captivating tale, we are left with a profound understanding of the human experience. "Threads of Resilience" serves as a mirror, reflecting our own triumphs and tribulations, reminding us of the extraordinary strength that resides within us all. It is a story that will stay with us, forever etched in our hearts, a testament to the resilience of the human spirit and the power of a life lived fully.

So, immerse yourself in the rich tapestry of Emily's life, and allow "Threads of Resilience: Weaving a Life Worth Living" to transport you on a journey that will leave you breathless, inspired, and forever changed.

# Chapter 1: Innocence Lost

Emily Williams, a child of boundless curiosity, was a beacon of light in the quaint town of Willowbrook. Her eyes, as vibrant as sapphires, glistened with an insatiable thirst for knowledge and a deep appreciation for the wonders that surrounded her. From the moment she could walk, she ventured into the lush woods that bordered her home, stepping into a realm where magic and reality intertwined.

As sunlight filtered through the verdant canopy, Emily's laughter echoed like birdsong, carrying the joy of discovery. Her tiny fingers traced the delicate petals of wildflowers, while her bare feet danced upon the moss-covered path, connecting her to the pulse of the Earth. Every rustle of leaves whispered secrets, every babbling brook invited her to explore further.

In those halcyon days of childhood, life was an endless adventure. Emily would spend hours lost in imaginary worlds, her imagination giving life to heroes and heroines, fierce dragons and friendly forest creatures. Willowbrook, with its charming cottages and winding lanes, served as the backdrop for her limitless dreams.

The aroma of freshly baked bread wafted through the air, mingling with the sweet fragrance of wildflowers. Friendly neighbors greeted her with warm smiles and stories of their own adventures, each tale adding another brushstroke to the vibrant canvas of her imagination. Willowbrook was not just a place—it was a sanctuary, a cocoon of love and endless possibilities that nurtured her curious spirit.

Through the lens of innocence, Emily saw the world as an intricate tapestry, woven with hues of wonder and excitement. Every dewdrop on a blade of grass, every twinkling star in the night sky, held the promise of a grand adventure waiting to unfold. The world, in all its complexity, was her playground, and she embraced it with open arms.

Little did she know then, as the sun cast its golden glow upon her face, that her journey would take her beyond the familiar woods of Willowbrook. It would lead her through valleys of pain and mountaintops of triumph, revealing the resilience that lay dormant within her soul.

But in those idyllic days, where the possibilities were as boundless as the sky above, Emily Williams stood on the precipice of a world waiting to be explored. With a heart full of wonder and eyes that sparkled with dreams, she set forth on a journey that would shape her destiny, leaving a mark on the tapestry of resilience that would inspire generations to come.

But fate, with its twisted sense of timing, had a cruel twist in store for young Emily. On that fateful autumn evening, when the air was heavy with a somber chill, tragedy lurked in the shadows, ready to shatter the fragile peace of her innocent existence. The sky hung low, pregnant with rain, as Emily's family home stood as a silent witness to what was about to unfold.

As the sun dipped below the horizon, a sinister flicker danced amidst the growing darkness. Flames, hungry and insatiable, engulfed the familiar walls that had once echoed with laughter and love. The crackling fire roared like a malevolent beast, swallowing cherished memories and hopes with its ravenous appetite. Orange tendrils reached out, clawing at the sky, painting a vivid, macabre portrait against the ebony canvas.

The air was thick with smoke, a haze that choked both lungs and spirits. The vibrant tapestry of Emily's life was torn apart, leaving her standing amidst the ruins, a solitary figure etched against the backdrop of devastation. Tears mixed with soot streaked down her soot-stained cheeks, her heart shattered into fragments, the weight of loss pressing upon her young shoulders.

"Mama! Papa!" Emily's anguished cry echoed through the night, a desperate plea to turn back time, to erase the tragedy that had stolen her loved ones from her embrace. But the only response was the haunting crackle of the fire, a cruel reminder of the cruel hand that fate had dealt her.

Alone and broken-hearted, Emily felt the weight of sorrow settle upon her like a leaden cloak. The world, once vibrant and full of wonder, now appeared muted and gray. Each breath she took was heavy with the burden of grief, and the shattered fragments of her innocence seemed irreparable.

In the midst of the smoldering wreckage, however, a spark of resilience flickered within Emily's anguished eyes. It was the indomitable spirit of a survivor, refusing to be consumed by despair. Amidst the ashes of her former life, she found the strength to rise, like a phoenix from the flames, her resolve burning brighter than ever before.

With trembling hands and a voice choked with determination, Emily vowed to rebuild her shattered existence. The flames that had stolen her family would not define her, but rather ignite within her the fierce fire of resilience. She would rise above the ashes, forging her own path, one that would carry her toward a future where triumph and resilience would intertwine, shaping the woman she was destined to become.

As Emily stood amidst the wreckage, her tears mixing with the rain, she whispered to the night sky, "I will not be defeated. I will rise. I will rebuild." And in that moment, a silent promise echoed in her soul—a promise to turn tragedy into fuel, to channel the pain into a force that would shape her future, and to find the strength to embrace the tapestry of resilience that awaited her, just beyond the horizon.

As the voracious flames consumed everything Emily held dear, they became a ravenous beast, insatiable in its hunger. The crackling inferno devoured precious memories, reducing them to ashes that danced on the gusts of wind. Each lick of the flames felt like a cruel caress, erasing the comforting warmth of her parents' embrace from her fingertips. She stood, transfixed in shock, amidst the charred ruins that were once the sanctuary of her childhood. The torrential rain cascaded down from the heavens, a mournful symphony that mirrored the tears streaming down her soot-streaked face.

Silent screams reverberated through the desolation, lost within the howling winds that carried the scent of destruction. The world around her crumbled, a once-familiar landscape transformed into a haunting tableau of devastation. The laughter that once echoed through the rooms now lay silenced, trapped in the memories of what once was. The rooms, now mere skeletons, whispered tales of love, laughter, and dreams shattered by the merciless flames.

The raindrops mingled with Emily's tears, tracing paths down her soot-covered cheeks, their mingled descent a poignant metaphor for her own grief. She tried to comprehend the enormity of her loss, grappling with the weight of an emptiness that threatened to engulf her entirely.

Amidst the wreckage, a whisper emerged from the depths of her soul, a voice that refused to be drowned out by the chaos. "I will not let this define me," she whispered, her words carried by the wind, a resolute declaration to the universe itself.

As she gazed upon the devastation, her eyes filled with a steely determination, an unyielding resolve that ignited within her like a flicker of hope. The ruins that surrounded her would not become a tomb, but rather a foundation upon which she would rebuild her shattered life. With trembling hands and raw determination, she vowed to rise from the ashes, breathing life into the charred remains of her dreams.

In the face of despair, Emily found an unexpected ally in the resolute beat of her own heart. It pulsed with a newfound strength, a beacon of resilience that would guide her through the darkest of nights. With each raindrop that mingled with her tears, a seed of resilience was planted, nourished by her determination to reclaim what was lost.

As she stood amidst the wreckage, her spirit unyielding, Emily whispered a promise to herself and to the universe, "I will rise again, stronger than before. These flames will not define me, but rather ignite within me a fire of resilience that will guide me towards a future where triumph and strength intertwine."

With every step she took away from the charred ruins, she carried within her a flicker of hope, a flame that burned brighter with each passing moment. The path ahead may have been obscured, but she knew deep within her soul that the journey towards rebuilding had just begun. And with her unwavering spirit as her guide, she would rise above the ashes, crafting a new chapter in her life—a chapter defined not by tragedy, but by the resolute strength of her spirit.

Emily, once cradled in the warmth of familial love, found herself abruptly thrust into a new reality—one fraught with uncertainty and a bone-deep loneliness that gnawed at her soul. The distant relatives who took her in were strangers with familiar faces, their hearts ill-prepared to offer the nurturing care she so desperately craved. Their home, once foreign, became a cold and hollow sanctuary that echoed with the ghosts of her past.

Days bled into months, and Emily navigated this unfamiliar landscape with a resilience that belied her tender years. While the world around her seemed devoid of color, her imagination became a vivid tapestry that unfurled with every beat of her heart. It was within the sanctuary of her mind that she sought solace, where dreams became her lifelines—fragile threads that tethered her to a reality of her own making.

In the confines of her small room, she painted breathtaking vistas upon the blank canvas of her mind. She conjured the vibrant hues of sunsets that caressed distant horizons, their fiery embrace casting away the shadows that clung to her spirit. The melodies of imagined symphonies swelled within her ears, harmonizing with the rhythm of her breathing, carrying her away to far-off lands where she could dance with abandon.

The isolation that surrounded her became a fertile ground for her dreams to take flight. With each stroke of her imagination, she built castles from whispers and weaved tales from strands of starlight. In the darkest corners of her solitude, she found companionship in the characters she brought to life—kindred spirits who embraced her as she truly was, with all her hopes, fears, and aspirations.

As she surrendered herself to the embrace of her dreams, her spirit soared beyond the confining walls that held her captive. In her mind's eye, she traversed sprawling landscapes, where the rustling of leaves became an orchestra, and the delicate touch of raindrops transformed into a symphony of life. She danced upon the precipice of possibility, her spirit unbound by the chains of her circumstances.

Through her imagination, Emily discovered a resilience that could not be extinguished. Her dreams became the compass guiding her through the labyrinth of loneliness, lighting the path towards a future where connection and belonging awaited her. And in those stolen moments of solace, she nurtured the flame of hope, safeguarding it with unwavering determination.

In the depths of her solitude, Emily whispered to the universe, her voice a quiet defiance against the cold indifference of her surroundings. "I may be alone, but I am not defeated. Within the sanctuary of my mind, I find solace, strength, and the unwavering belief that my dreams will carry me through."

And as she surrendered herself to the enchantment of her imagination, Emily dared to believe that the world beyond her door held wonders yet to be discovered—a world where resilience would blossom into resilience, where the ache of loneliness would be replaced by the symphony of connection, and where her dreams, like seeds sown in fertile soil, would bloom into a reality as vibrant and breathtaking as the worlds she created within herself.

Haunted by the ghostly remnants of her past, Emily carried the weight of her loss like an invisible burden, each step she took an echo of the sorrow etched into her soul. The spark that once danced in her eyes flickered, dimmed by the shadows that clung to her spirit. The once-vibrant child became a mere whisper of herself, withdrawn and cocooned within a veil of sorrow. Her laughter, once a symphony that filled the air, was now a muted melody, confined to the chambers of her heart.

Every day, she navigated the world with a heaviness that seemed impossible to shake. The memories of the warmth of her parents' love, their gentle touch and comforting words, lingered like a bittersweet symphony in her mind. The rooms of her heart echoed with their absence, their absence a constant reminder of the void that could never be filled.

Yet, amidst the darkness that threatened to engulf her, a flicker of resilience burned within Emily, a flame that refused to be extinguished. It was the indomitable spirit of a survivor, a whisper from the depths of her being that urged her to keep moving forward, to defy the weight of her sorrows.

In the stillness of the night, when the world lay shrouded in darkness, Emily dared to confront her pain. She would sit by the window, gazing at the moon as it bathed the world in its pale glow, searching for solace in the celestial canvas above. The moon, with its silent luminescence, became her confidante, bearing witness to the tears she shed and the unspoken conversations she longed to have.

"Are you there, Mama? Papa?" Emily would whisper into the night, her voice carrying a longing that transcended time and space. In the silence that followed, she imagined their whispers of love carried by the breeze, their ethereal embrace offering comfort to her aching heart.

Through the solitude, Emily discovered an inner strength she never knew she possessed. It was a strength born from the ashes of her shattered past, tempered by the trials she had endured. She refused to allow her sorrow to define her, to be swallowed whole by the depths of her grief. Instead, she sought solace in the whispered encouragement of her own spirit, a voice that reminded her of the resilience that lay dormant within.

As the flicker of resilience burned brighter within her, Emily's gaze shifted from the shadows of her past to the horizon of possibilities. The ghosts that haunted her became the fuel that stoked the fires of her determination. With each breath she took, she reclaimed fragments of herself, piecing together the mosaic of her spirit.

In those moments of quiet introspection, Emily made a silent vow to honor her past by embracing the future with open arms. The weight of her loss would not define her, but rather serve as a reminder of the strength she carried within. She would rise from the depths of her sorrow, shedding the cloak of grief, and emerge as a testament to the resilience of the human spirit.

With the flicker of resilience burning ever brighter, Emily whispered to the stars that adorned the night sky, "I may carry the weight of my loss, but it will not break me. In the face of adversity, I will rise, reclaiming my laughter, igniting the flame of my spirit, and finding solace in the beauty that still exists within and around me."

And in that moment, as the moon bathed her tear-streaked face in its gentle glow, Emily began to glimpse the transformative power of resilience—a force that would carry her through the darkest nights and guide her toward a future where healing, growth, and triumph awaited her.

With unwavering determination and an unyielding spirit, Emily weathered the tumultuous years of adolescence, a journey fraught with stumbling blocks and hidden perils. It was a time when uncertainty mingled with the longing for stability, and the echoes of her past reverberated through the corridors of her being.

In the hallowed sanctuary of her room, Emily sought refuge within the boundless realms of books. She became a seeker of stories, diving headfirst into the pages that whispered promises of escape and inspiration. With each turn of a page, she felt herself transported to distant lands, where heroes and heroines battled against formidable odds, mirroring the struggles she faced in her own life.

Within the cocoon of imagination, she discovered fragments of hope and courage, nestled within the folds of every chapter. The characters she encountered became friends, their journeys intertwining with her own. From the wisdom of sages to the resilience of underdogs, their stories weaved a tapestry of lessons, imparting to her the strength to persevere.

In the world of literature, Emily found solace, drawing comfort from the ink-stained pages that held the keys to unlocking her own potential. With each book she devoured, she felt the chains of her circumstances loosen, as if a chorus of voices whispered encouragement in her ear. These fictional realms became the forge where her resilience was tempered, where her desire to rise above her circumstances grew stronger with each tale of triumph against adversity.

She would spend countless hours nestled in her favorite reading nook, her fingers tracing the well-worn spines of her beloved books. As her eyes traced the words written by distant authors, her imagination set sail on uncharted seas, guided by the compass of her dreams. Through the power of storytelling, she discovered a kinship with the characters who had triumphed against insurmountable odds, finding solace in their victories, and solace in the knowledge that she, too, could forge her own path.

Sometimes, she would lose herself in the poetic prose of a classic novel, where intricate descriptions painted vivid landscapes within her mind. The scent of blooming flowers would waft through her thoughts, the crispness of the air would send shivers down her spine, and the roar of crashing waves would reverberate within her very being. She was transported beyond the confines of her small room, her spirit expanding to encompass the vastness of the literary worlds she inhabited.

Other times, she would immerse herself in gripping narratives that unfolded like cinematic masterpieces. The dialogue would come alive within her imagination, the characters' voices resonating as if they were standing beside her, sharing their triumphs, fears, and hopes. She would laugh with them, cry with them, and find solace in their shared humanity.

And with each book she devoured, Emily felt the embers of her resilience burn brighter. The stories she absorbed, the lessons she gleaned, all coalesced into a fire that fueled her determination to transcend her circumstances. She realized that the power of words was not merely confined to the pages but had the capacity to shape her reality, to mold her into the person she aspired to be.

In those moments of literary immersion, Emily whispered to the universe, "These stories are not just ink on paper, but beacons of hope and inspiration. They remind me that the pen is mightier than the sword, and that within me lies a reservoir of strength waiting to be unleashed. I will rise above the limitations of my past, armed with the courage bestowed upon me by these stories."

And as she closed the final chapter of each book, Emily felt a renewed sense of purpose. She emerged from her literary odysseys with a fervor to write her own story, to become the author of her destiny. With each stroke of her pen, she would etch her dreams onto the blank pages of her life, crafting a narrative filled with resilience, courage, and triumph.

For within the pages of the countless worlds she explored, Emily discovered that the power to shape her own story resided within her heart and mind. And armed with the lessons learned from the characters she held dear, she set forth on a new chapter, ready to conquer the challenges that lay ahead and to pen a tale of her own—one that would inspire others to find their own fragments of hope and courage within the narratives of their lives.

As the tendrils of time wove their tapestry, Emily blossomed into a young woman, her spirit ablaze with a fervent yearning for self-discovery. Like a caged bird beating its wings against the confines of its prison, she longed to break free from the suffocating grasp of her small town, where echoes of her past reverberated through every street and whispered in the wind.

In the depths of her heart, a hunger for adventure stirred, a magnetic force that tugged relentlessly at her restless spirit. Willowbrook, with its quaint charm and familiar faces, no longer held the allure it once did. The boundaries of her world had become a mere whisper, easily penetrated by the winds of curiosity that swept through her being.

Her dreams carried her to distant horizons, where uncharted lands awaited her footprints. The world beyond the boundaries of Willowbrook beckoned, its siren song resonating with her soul. She yearned to traverse landscapes unknown, to drink from the fountains of discovery, and to bask in the embrace of cultures as vibrant and diverse as the colors of a sunset.

With a heart brimming with anticipation, Emily stood at the crossroads of her destiny. Her eyes, alight with determination, gazed beyond the familiar, seeking the unknown. The air crackled with possibility, as if the universe itself whispered secrets of what lay beyond the horizon.

A pivotal moment arrived, like a fleeting comet streaking across the night sky. Emily gathered her courage and embraced the unknown, bidding farewell to the familiar faces that had shaped her past. In the twilight of her departure, her footsteps echoed with a resolute rhythm, each stride a testament to her determination to forge her own path.

As she ventured beyond the borders of Willowbrook, the world unfolded before her like a vast tapestry of wonders. The scent of foreign spices mingled with the vibrant hues of bustling markets, while the symphony of languages danced in her ears, a melodious harmony that celebrated the diversity of human existence.

From the labyrinthine streets of ancient cities to the serene serenade of sun-kissed beaches, Emily found herself immersed in a kaleidoscope of experiences. She drank the nectar of adventure, savoring every drop as it cascaded down her throat, invigorating her spirit and illuminating the depths of her soul.

Her encounters became the brushstrokes that painted the canvas of her journey—a chance meeting with a wise old sage atop a misty mountaintop, whose words carried the weight of ancient wisdom; a heart-stopping chase through the bustling alleys of a vibrant bazaar, the pulse of adrenaline echoing in her veins; and a soul-stirring sunset that painted the sky in hues of gold and crimson, a symphony of colors that whispered of the beauty and transience of life.

In those moments of exhilaration and introspection, Emily discovered that the world was vast, intricate, and awe-inspiring. Her quest for self-discovery intertwined with her thirst for adventure, each step an opportunity to uncover hidden fragments of herself, to push the boundaries of her limitations, and to carve her name upon the tapestry of her existence.

And as she stood on the precipice of her own evolution, a smile played upon Emily's lips. The call of the unknown had transformed her, infusing her spirit with a newfound sense of purpose and an insatiable hunger for life's myriad treasures. The restless heart that had once yearned for escape had found solace in the intoxicating dance of exploration.

In a whispered declaration to the universe, Emily spoke, her voice carrying the echoes of the winds that had guided her. "I am a wanderer, a seeker of truths hidden beneath foreign skies. My spirit soars on wings woven from the fabric of my dreams. With each step, I discover fragments of myself, untangling the tapestry of my past and weaving a future painted with the hues of possibility."

And so, she ventured forth, her heart alight with the flame of adventure. The road ahead was uncharted, winding through valleys of uncertainty and peaks of exhilaration. But Emily, armed with her indomitable spirit and an insatiable thirst for life, embraced the unknown, knowing that within its depths lay the secrets of her own becoming.

With a bittersweet blend of trepidation and anticipation, Emily stood at the threshold of her childhood home, her gaze fixed upon the horizon that beckoned her forward. The weight of memories clung to her like a familiar embrace, tugging at her heartstrings, but the allure of the unknown whispered promises of liberation.

As she shouldered her backpack, its worn fabric a testament to the adventures it had witnessed, Emily felt a surge of energy coursing through her veins. It was a mélange of nerves and excitement, an intoxicating blend that fueled her determination to chase her dreams.

With each step she took, the familiar streets of Willowbrook receded into a blur of fading images, replaced by the untamed wilderness of the open road. The world unfurled before her like a magnificent tapestry, its threads woven with opportunities, challenges, and unforeseen wonders.

As the sun kissed the horizon, casting a golden hue upon the landscape, Emily's resolve grew stronger. The road stretched out before her, an uncharted path veiled in mystery. It whispered tales of distant lands, diverse cultures, and experiences that would shape her in ways she could not yet fathom.

The air hummed with anticipation, carrying with it the symphony of the unknown. With each passing mile, Emily's spirit soared, unburdened by the weight of the past, liberated by the infinite possibilities that lay ahead. She embraced the uncertainty, for it was in the unscripted moments that the true essence of life revealed itself.

Amidst the breathtaking vistas and the hidden corners of the world, Emily encountered fellow wanderers on their own quest for meaning. Their paths converged in transient encounters and serendipitous meetings, forging connections that would leave an indelible mark upon her soul.

In the gentle glow of a campfire beneath a star-studded sky, conversations blossomed like wildflowers in a meadow. Strangers became companions, and stories intertwined, carrying the collective wisdom of lives lived and lessons learned. They shared laughter, tears, and insights, their words weaving a tapestry of human experience that resonated deep within Emily's being.

Within the intimate exchanges of shared dreams and whispered aspirations, Emily found solace. The camaraderie of kindred spirits illuminated her path, offering support and companionship in the face of challenges. They became a constellation of guiding stars, lighting the way when doubt threatened to dim her resolve.

And as the road stretched onward, lined with towering mountains and winding rivers, Emily's spirit expanded to embrace the vastness of the world. She reveled in the symphony of unfamiliar languages that danced upon her ears, the fragrant spices that tickled her senses, and the kaleidoscope of cultures that painted her journey with vibrant hues.

There were moments of doubt, of weariness, when the weight of her backpack seemed too heavy to bear. But with each obstacle overcome, Emily discovered reservoirs of strength and resilience she never knew she possessed. She found that the bumps on the road were not stumbling blocks, but stepping stones that propelled her forward, shaping her into the person she was destined to become.

In the quiet solitude of her thoughts, Emily would often reflect upon the transformative power of her journey. With a twinkle in her eyes, she would whisper to the wind, "I may have bid farewell to the comfort of the familiar, but in exchange, I have gained a world of experiences, a tapestry of memories, and a deeper understanding of myself."

And so, she ventured on, driven by an unwavering determination to find her place in the vast mosaic of existence. The road stretched out, unending and full of promise, as Emily, armed with nothing more than her dreams and the fire in her heart, embraced the adventure that awaited her with open arms.

Little did Emily know that her path would be a labyrinthine maze, fraught with unforeseen twists and treacherous turns. The road she tread upon would demand her resilience, pushing her to the very limits of her strength. But she carried within her an indomitable spirit, a flame that flickered defiantly in the face of adversity.

As Emily journeyed further into the depths of the unknown, challenges arose like formidable mountains blocking her way. The winds of change howled, threatening to extinguish the fire within her. Yet, with every obstacle that threatened to break her stride, she stood tall, her eyes gleaming with unwavering determination.

Life, in its infinite complexity, had tested Emily at a tender age, carving scars upon her soul. But she refused to be defined by tragedy. Each scar became a testament to her resilience, a symbol of her ability to rise from the ashes of despair. She had tasted the bitterness of loss, but it only fueled her hunger for a life lived on her own terms.

Through heartbreak and disappointment, Emily learned the art of perseverance. She embraced the pain as an integral part of her journey, understanding that it was through the cracks in her heart that the light would seep in, illuminating the path before her. In the face of adversity, she discovered the extraordinary strength that resided within her, a force that propelled her forward even when the weight of the world threatened to crush her spirit.

With each step she took, Emily's resolve grew stronger. She refused to be a mere victim of circumstance, instead choosing to rewrite her story, to redefine her own narrative. Life had thrown its harshest blows at her, but she refused to surrender to its whims.

In moments of doubt, when the shadows of her past threatened to engulf her, Emily would seek solace in her own reflection. "I am not defined by the tragedies I have endured," she would whisper to herself, her voice carrying the echoes of her determination. "I am defined by how I rise from the ashes, by the strength I summon in the face of adversity."

The world around her may have seen her scars as blemishes, reminders of a painful past, but Emily saw them as badges of honor. Each mark told a story of survival, of a spirit that refused to be broken. They were reminders of the battles she had fought and the battles she would continue to fight, a testament to her unwavering resolve.

As she forged ahead, navigating the winding roads of uncertainty, Emily encountered others who bore their own scars, their own stories of resilience. Their paths intersected, forming a tapestry of shared experiences and collective strength. In their company, Emily found kinship, a support system that lifted her up when her steps faltered.

And as she faced the challenges that lay ahead, Emily's spirit burned with a fierce determination. She knew that life was a relentless master, but she was an unwavering student. She would face each trial head-on, armed with the knowledge that scars did not define weakness, but rather, they were the marks of a survivor.

With unwavering resolve, Emily whispered into the wind, her voice carried on its currents, "I am stronger than the wounds of my past, and I will continue to rise, to forge my own path amidst the challenges that come my way."

And so, with scars as her armor and resilience as her shield, Emily strode forward, ready to conquer the untamed wilderness of life, unyielding in her pursuit of a future that transcended the boundaries of tragedy.

As Emily ventured into the vast expanse of the world, her footsteps etched new pathways upon the tapestry of her life. The landscape unfolded before her like a canvas painted with breathtaking vistas and untamed wilderness. Each step brought her closer to the unknown, where hidden treasures awaited her arrival.

In her wanderings, Emily stumbled upon unexpected allies, their presence like serendipitous encounters orchestrated by a benevolent universe. From the weathered storyteller on a park bench, whose tales wove threads of wisdom into the very fabric of her being, to the nomadic soul who shared a campfire and ignited her imagination with stories of distant lands and adventures, each encounter left an indelible mark upon her journey.

Their voices intertwined with hers, their stories mingling with hers, creating a symphony of shared experiences that resonated deep within her core. With each interaction, she discovered the beauty of human connection, the power of compassion and understanding to bridge the gaps between strangers. They became her confidants, her pillars of support, and her partners in the pursuit of a life lived with purpose.

Amidst the breathtaking landscapes and the untamed wilderness, Emily confronted her deepest fears, those lurking in the shadows of her subconscious. She peered into the abyss of self-doubt, daring to face the demons that whispered tales of inadequacy and failure. With every act of courage, she unraveled the threads that bound her, liberating herself from the shackles of fear.

There were moments when the weight of uncertainty threatened to overwhelm her, when the path ahead seemed obscured by mist and doubt. But in those moments, Emily turned to the resilience that had carried her through the darkest chapters of her life. She summoned her inner strength, refusing to be deterred by the whispers of doubt that echoed in her mind.

The transformative power of resilience unfolded before her eyes, revealing the depths of her own potential. She witnessed her own capacity to overcome, to adapt, and to thrive in the face of adversity. The challenges she encountered became catalysts for growth, propelling her forward on her quest for self-discovery.

As she ventured deeper into the unknown, Emily marveled at the tapestry of her own resilience, woven from the threads of her experiences. She saw how each setback had fortified her spirit, how every obstacle had sharpened her resolve. In the crucible of life's trials, she discovered her own untapped reserves of strength and resilience, emerging from each battle stronger, wiser, and more determined than before.

With each step, she whispered words of encouragement to herself, her voice mingling with the wind. "I am a weaver of my own destiny, a master of my own resilience. The challenges that come my way are opportunities for growth, and I embrace them with open arms."

And so, Emily ventured onward, guided by an unwavering spirit and an insatiable hunger for the unknown. With each encounter, each fear confronted, and each lesson learned, she unraveled the tapestry of her life, discovering the extraordinary power of resilience to shape her journey. And in doing so, she wove a story that would inspire others to embark on their own quests for resilience and self-discovery.

# Chapter 2: Battling Demons

Emily's footsteps reverberated through the labyrinthine streets of the bustling metropolis, a symphony of determination amidst the cacophony of city life. The towering skyscrapers loomed overhead, their glass facades reflecting the vibrant lights that illuminated the night. The pulsating energy of the city pulsed through her veins, filling her with a sense of exhilaration and possibility.

Gone were the quaint, tree-lined roads of Willowbrook, replaced by the ceaseless rhythm of car horns and the hurried footsteps of passersby. The air was thick with the scent of ambition and opportunity, an intoxicating blend that drew her deeper into its embrace. She walked with purpose, her eyes fixed on the horizon, where dreams danced on the edges of her vision.

The urban landscape, with its towering buildings and bustling streets, was a stark contrast to the serene beauty of her childhood home. Yet, Emily welcomed the change, craving the anonymity and the chance to reinvent herself. It was an opportunity to leave behind the painful memories that had haunted her, to shed the weight of the past, and embark on a new chapter of her life.

As she navigated the labyrinth of city life, Emily felt a surge of liberation. Here, amidst the concrete and steel, she could redefine herself, free from the judgment and expectations of a small town. The city was a vast canvas, waiting for her to paint her own vibrant strokes upon its surface.

In the midst of the bustling streets, she discovered pockets of solace—the tranquil parks, hidden cafes, and winding alleys that offered fleeting moments of respite from the urban chaos. In those quiet spaces, she would pause, letting the city's pulse fade into the background, and breathe in the promise of new beginnings.

Amongst the throngs of strangers, Emily would occasionally catch fragments of conversation drifting on the wind. Snippets of dreams and ambitions, whispered hopes and whispered confessions, painted the air with an ethereal sense of possibility. They fueled her own aspirations, igniting a fire within her that burned brighter with each passing day.

The city became her companion, a relentless mentor that pushed her to the limits of her abilities. She navigated the web of opportunities, daring to chase after her dreams with unwavering resolve. Through late nights and early mornings, she toiled, her determination unwavering, her spirit unyielding.

Amidst the pulsating energy of the city, Emily found herself face to face with the mirror of her own reflection. In its glassy surface, she saw the transformation that had taken hold within her—a woman of resilience, strength, and unwavering determination. The pain of her past had shaped her, but it did not define her. She was an architect of her own destiny, weaving a future that defied the shadows of her past.

And so, with each step she took, Emily embraced the vibrant chaos of the city, embracing its rhythm as her own. The echoes of her footsteps carried a new melody, a symphony of resilience, and an anthem of hope. The city, with all its complexities and contradictions, became her muse, propelling her towards the grand stage where her dreams awaited their moment to shine.

In the dimly lit streets, as the city's pulse beat in harmony with her own, Emily whispered to herself, her voice resolute amidst the urban symphony, "This city will not break me. I will conquer its challenges, carve my own path, and leave an indelible mark upon its streets."

And so, she pressed forward, a solitary figure navigating the urban tapestry, her footsteps a testament to her unwavering spirit and unyielding determination. In the heart of the city, Emily would rewrite her story, reclaim her power, and embrace the boundless possibilities that awaited her.

In this new environment, the city's vibrant energy became a double-edged sword for Emily. It seduced her with its pulsating rhythm and dazzling lights, drawing her into its labyrinthine embrace. Yet, within the shadows that danced beneath the neon glow, darker temptations awaited, lurking like sirens eager to ensnare the unsuspecting.

As Emily ventured deeper into the city's underbelly, she discovered a world teeming with desire and desperation. A surreal kaleidoscope of characters and vices emerged from the shadows, their faces etched with the weight of their own battles. In dimly lit alleyways, whispered conversations wove a tangled web of secrets and deceit, and the air grew heavy with the scent of substances that promised temporary oblivion.

At first, the allure of escape beckoned to Emily, a tantalizing respite from the pain that still lingered within her. It was in the depths of her vulnerability that the insidious grip of addiction took hold, slowly tightening its suffocating tendrils around her. What began as an innocent curiosity morphed into a dangerous dance, where her cravings clashed with her willpower, leaving her trapped in a cycle of longing and self-destruction.

Haunted by the demons that whispered seductive lies, Emily found herself spiraling into a darkness she never thought possible. The vibrant streets that once promised freedom now became a labyrinth of temptation, where the line between pleasure and destruction blurred with each passing day. She witnessed the toll addiction took on those around her—the hollow eyes, the trembling hands, and the shattered dreams—serving as cautionary tales that wove their way into her consciousness.

It was in the depths of her darkest moments that Emily confronted the harsh reality of her choices. She stood at the precipice of a life derailed, her spirit weary from the battle within. Yet, within the darkness, a flicker of resilience burned, reminding her of the strength she had once harnessed to overcome adversity.

In a moment of clarity amidst the chaos, Emily found herself face to face with a stranger—a weathered soul who had walked a similar path and emerged on the other side. Their eyes met, a silent understanding passing between them, as if their shared experiences transcended words. With compassion in their voice, the stranger extended a hand of support, offering a lifeline that had the potential to alter the course of Emily's life.

"You have a fire within you, Emily," the stranger said, their voice weathered but filled with hope. "I've seen it before, in the eyes of those who have fought the same battles you face. You are capable of rising above this darkness, of reclaiming your power and rewriting your story."

The stranger's words struck a chord deep within Emily's soul, resonating with a truth she had forgotten. She realized that her journey was not defined by the mistakes she had made, but by her capacity for growth and transformation. The allure of addiction had clouded her vision, but now, in the face of a glimmering possibility, she could envision a different path.

With determination burning in her eyes, Emily made a choice—a choice to break free from the grip of addiction, to reclaim her identity, and to rewrite the narrative of her life. It would not be an easy journey, but she knew that within her resided the strength and resilience to overcome the demons that threatened to consume her.

As she took the stranger's outstretched hand, she whispered a vow to herself, her voice filled with newfound resolve. "I will defy the darkness, for I am more than the temptations that seek to confine me. I will reclaim my power and forge a path of healing and redemption."

And so, with the stranger by her side, Emily embarked on a new chapter of her life—a chapter filled with grit, vulnerability, and the unwavering determination to overcome the shadows that had threatened to consume her. The city, once a catalyst for her downfall, would now bear witness to her resilience as she fought to reclaim her place in the world.

In the face of adversity, Emily discovered an inner strength she never knew existed. The journey ahead would be arduous, fraught with pitfalls and moments of doubt. But armed with the knowledge that she was more than her past mistakes, Emily walked the path of recovery, step by painstaking step, towards a future where hope and redemption awaited her.

Seeking solace from the persistent ache of loss, Emily found herself drawn into a perilous dance with substances that whispered promises of temporary oblivion. In the depths of her grief, she sought refuge in the numbing embrace they offered, their seductive allure becoming a siren's call that beckoned her deeper into a labyrinth of self-destruction.

As the weight of her sorrow threatened to consume her, Emily's once-clear path became obscured by a haze of smoke and blurred lines. The friends she had once cherished morphed into enablers, their own pain intertwined with hers, their intentions masked by their own desperate pursuit of solace.

In the dimly lit corners of her existence, Emily's true essence became eclipsed by the shadows that clung to her. Her laughter, once a resounding melody, became muted, stifled by the smokescreen of her addiction. The dreams she once held dear faded into distant whispers, drowned out by the clamor of her destructive habits.

But even within the depths of her descent, a glimmer of self-awareness flickered like a distant star. Through the haze, a voice emerged—the voice of a stranger, a guardian angel disguised as a passerby. Their words were laced with equal parts concern and urgency, piercing through the fog that clouded Emily's judgment.

"You are losing yourself, Emily," the stranger whispered, their voice laden with the weight of empathy. "The substances that promise solace are stealing your light. You are more than this—more than the shadows that threaten to consume you."

Emily's gaze met the stranger's, and for a moment, time stood still. In that fleeting exchange, a seed of hope was planted, nurturing the ember of resilience that still smoldered within her. It was a pivotal moment—a choice between surrendering to the abyss or mustering the strength to reclaim her identity.

The journey to reclaim her life would not be without its trials. The allure of numbness would continue to beckon, and the treacherous path of recovery would test her resolve. But armed with the knowledge that she was worthy of a brighter future, Emily mustered the strength to take the first step—a step away from the suffocating grip of addiction, and towards a life of healing and redemption.

With each passing day, Emily peeled back the layers of her addiction, confronting the painful memories and unresolved emotions that had led her astray. She sought support in the embrace of recovery groups, where she discovered a network of individuals who understood her struggles, their stories intertwining with hers in a tapestry of shared experience.

The road to recovery was marked by peaks and valleys, moments of triumph and setbacks. But with each milestone achieved, Emily reclaimed a fragment of herself that had been lost along the way. The laughter that had once been stifled rang out once more, carrying the sweet melody of newfound freedom. The dreams she had buried deep within her soul resurfaced, fueled by the realization that she was capable of crafting a future defined by strength and purpose.

Emily's journey was not one of erasing her past, but rather of reconciling with it—a testament to the indomitable human spirit and its capacity for redemption. Through the wreckage of her addiction, she emerged as a beacon of resilience, a testament to the power of self-discovery and the unwavering determination to rewrite one's own narrative.

And as Emily walked the path of recovery, she knew that her story was not only hers to tell but also a testament to the resilience that resided within each individual. Her triumph over adversity served as a reminder that even in the darkest of moments, the human spirit possesses an innate ability to heal, to rise above, and to embrace the fragments of resilience that lie within us all.

Days blended into nights, their boundaries blurred by the haze of self-destructive behavior that held Emily captive. The once-vibrant dreams that had danced through her mind now withered beneath the weight of her addiction, their colors muted, their magic obscured. The sparkle in her eyes, once a testament to her boundless curiosity, dimmed, replaced by a vacant stare that seemed to gaze into a void.

Yet, buried deep within the recesses of her soul, a flicker of resilience persisted—a tiny ember that refused to be extinguished. It burned with a quiet determination, an unwavering flame that whispered reminders of her true essence amidst the cacophony of her addiction.

One moonlit night, as Emily found herself perched on the edge of a precipice, contemplating the depths to which she had fallen, a voice from within rumbled with a newfound strength. It emerged as a gentle but insistent call, urging her to remember who she was beyond the suffocating grip of her vices.

"You are not defined by your mistakes," the voice resonated, carrying with it the echoes of her forgotten dreams and aspirations. "Within you lies a resilience that can transcend this darkness. Embrace the flicker within and let it guide you back to the light."

Emily's heart trembled as the words reverberated through her being. In that moment, the choice to either surrender to the abyss or summon the strength to reclaim her true self lay before her like a crossroads. It was a battle waged in the depths of her soul, the outcome holding the key to her liberation.

A surge of determination coursed through her veins, breathing life into her dormant spirit. With a resolute gaze fixed on the horizon, Emily took her first faltering steps towards a path of healing and redemption. Each footfall was a declaration of defiance against the darkness that had threatened to consume her.

The journey to reclaim her identity was fraught with challenges, a labyrinth of trials that tested her resolve at every turn. But with each hurdle she overcame, the flicker within her grew brighter, its light casting aside the shadows that clung to her like tendrils of smoke.

In the embrace of support groups and therapy sessions, Emily found solace and understanding. Her fellow warriors, each carrying their own scars and battles, became pillars of strength and inspiration. Their collective stories intertwined, weaving a tapestry of resilience that served as a beacon of hope in the darkness.

With the passage of time, the hazy days and restless nights transformed into moments of clarity and purpose. Emily's laughter, once silenced, returned like a gentle breeze, bringing warmth to the hearts of those around her. The dreams that had been buried deep within her soul emerged once more, shimmering with renewed vitality.

As Emily walked the path of recovery, she discovered the transformative power of self-discovery. She shed the shackles of her addiction, embracing her scars as reminders of the battles she had fought and the strength she had gained. Each day was a testament to her unwavering spirit, a testament to the human capacity for redemption and renewal.

And so, the flicker of resilience that had burned within Emily, once fragile and faint, grew into an inferno that illuminated her path. It guided her towards a future where she could not only heal her own wounds but also offer hope to others who found themselves trapped in the clutches of darkness.

Emily's journey was not just a story of survival; it was a symphony of resilience, a testament to the enduring power of the human spirit. And as she embraced her newfound purpose, she vowed to share her story, to be a guiding light for those who had lost their way.

For within the depths of every soul lies a flicker of resilience, waiting to be ignited—a reminder that no matter how fierce the storm, there is always a chance for redemption, healing, and the rekindling of the spark within.

One fateful night, as Emily aimlessly wandered the deserted streets, the air thick with melancholy, a figure emerged from the shadows like a guardian angel. His name was Daniel, a man whose rugged exterior hinted at the battles he had fought and the victories he had won. The weary lines etched upon his face bore witness to the depths of his own journey towards redemption.

Their eyes met, and in that instant, a profound understanding passed between them. Daniel saw his reflection in Emily's tear-stained visage, recognizing the torment and anguish that consumed her. He approached her with cautious steps, his voice a gentle salve to her wounded spirit.

"I've been where you are," Daniel murmured, his voice tinged with a blend of empathy and hope. "I've felt the weight of despair and the relentless pull of addiction. But I also know that within you lies a strength beyond measure—a strength that can guide you back to the light."

Emily's heart trembled at the sincerity in his voice, her gaze locked with his as if seeking solace within his gaze. His words resonated deep within her, touching upon a flicker of hope she had almost forgotten existed.

"Who are you?" she whispered, her voice fragile yet laced with curiosity.

Daniel's lips curled into a bittersweet smile, the ghosts of his past momentarily flickering across his eyes. "I am someone who understands," he replied, his voice carrying the weight of his own journey. "Someone who believes that no one is beyond redemption. And if you allow me, I can be a guiding light on your path to healing."

Tears welled in Emily's eyes, mingling with the shadows that had haunted her for far too long. A tremor of vulnerability coursed through her, mingled with a glimmer of hope she had thought had long abandoned her.

She nodded, her voice barely above a whisper. "Show me the way," she pleaded, a newfound determination seeping into her words.

With that unspoken promise, their journeys intertwined, bound by the common thread of resilience. Daniel became her mentor, guiding her through the labyrinth of recovery with unwavering support and unwritten understanding. He shared his own triumphs and setbacks, painting vivid portraits of redemption and offering her the tools to rebuild her shattered world.

Together, they navigated the jagged edges of temptation and the treacherous pitfalls that lined the path of recovery. Their bond strengthened, fortified by shared experiences and an unspoken language of compassion.

As Emily emerged from the depths of her addiction, she found not only the strength to heal but also a purpose rooted in helping others. With Daniel's guidance, she became a beacon of hope for those who still battled their own demons. Her journey became a testament to the transformative power of human connection, reminding others that they were not alone in their struggles.

And so, as the moon cast its gentle glow upon their shared path, Emily and Daniel continued their journey, their footsteps leaving behind imprints of resilience and the unyielding belief that even in the darkest of nights, a glimmer of hope can illuminate the way forward.

Daniel's kind eyes held a glimmer of understanding, like two embers flickering amidst the vast darkness. In the moonlight, his outstretched hand offered a lifeline of hope, the calloused skin a testament to the battles he had fought and the scars he carried. It was in his touch that Emily felt a surge of energy, as if the universe conspired to lead her to this pivotal moment.

With a voice softened by the weight of his own story, Daniel began to weave a tapestry of redemption and resilience. His words danced in the air, painting vibrant hues on the canvas of Emily's imagination. Each syllable carried the weight of his past, the vulnerability of a soul laid bare.

"I've journeyed through the darkest corridors of addiction," Daniel spoke, his voice laced with quiet determination. "I've felt the pull of despair and the crushing weight of regret. But I've also tasted the sweetness of recovery, the triumph of reclaiming my own life."

Emily's heart trembled as Daniel's words penetrated the fortress of her pain. A surge of hope coursed through her veins, mingling with the echoes of his promises. In his narrative, she glimpsed the possibility of a brighter future, of a life filled with purpose and fulfillment.

As he wove his tale, Daniel painted vivid scenes of transformation and triumph. He spoke of battles won against the relentless grip of addiction, of the unbreakable spirit that resides within every shattered soul. His words became a beacon of light, illuminating the path that lay ahead for Emily.

"With every step towards recovery," Daniel continued, his voice carrying a symphony of resilience, "you will discover a strength within you that you never knew existed. It will be a journey of self-discovery, of healing the wounds that have held you captive. But always remember, you are not alone. I will walk beside you, offering support and guidance, until you find the strength to stand on your own."

Emily felt her breath catch, her spirit soaring on the wings of Daniel's words. She looked into his eyes, a newfound determination gleaming in her own. "I'm ready," she declared, her voice carrying the weight of her resolve. "I'm ready to embrace a life free from the chains of addiction, ready to rebuild myself from the fragments of resilience that remain."

Daniel's smile was both tender and triumphant, a reflection of the battles he had fought and the victories he had won. In that moment, their shared journey began, a tapestry of redemption and renewal unfurling before them.

Together, they would navigate the treacherous terrain of recovery, traversing the valleys of temptation and scaling the mountains of self-doubt. Daniel's words would be the compass that guided her, his unwavering support a lifeline amidst the storms of doubt.

And so, hand in hand, Emily and Daniel embarked on their shared odyssey, their footsteps resonating with the echoes of resilience. With each passing day, their connection grew stronger, their stories interwoven in a tapestry of hope and possibility.

As the sun painted the horizon with hues of gold and crimson, they set their sights on a future brighter than they had ever imagined. Together, they would rewrite the narrative of their lives, casting aside the shadows of addiction and embracing the boundless potential that lay within.

In the embrace of their shared journey, Emily discovered not only the strength to heal herself but also the power to inspire others. She would become a beacon of hope, a living testament to the transformative power of resilience and the unbreakable spirit that resides within us all.

And so, as they walked hand in hand, the winds whispered promises of a brighter future, carrying their stories to the corners of the world, igniting a spark of hope in the hearts of those who needed it most.

With Daniel's unwavering support, Emily embarked on the treacherous journey of recovery, determined to confront her addiction head-on. The path ahead was an uphill battle, strewn with obstacles that tested her resolve at every turn. The specter of withdrawal loomed over her, a relentless shadow that taunted her with its insidious whispers.

As Emily grappled with the grip of addiction, she experienced the tumultuous waves of withdrawal crashing against the shores of her being. The nights were the hardest, as her body convulsed with cravings and her mind played tricks on her weary soul. In those moments of despair, Daniel's voice became her lifeline, a constant reminder of the strength she possessed within.

"I know it's difficult," Daniel whispered, his voice infused with empathy. "But remember, you are stronger than the grip of addiction. The pain you feel now is temporary, a testament to your courage in breaking free from its clutches."

Emily clung to his words like a castaway clinging to a life raft in a stormy sea. She held onto his guidance as if it were a precious compass leading her out of the darkness. Through the sleepless nights and the relentless cravings, she summoned every ounce of strength within her, refusing to let the addiction define her.

But the road to recovery was not without its setbacks. There were moments when the weight of the world seemed too heavy to bear, and she stumbled along the way. Each relapse threatened to derail her progress, whispering doubts into her weary ears. But with Daniel's steady presence by her side, she found the resilience to dust herself off and continue the journey.

"I believe in you," Daniel said, his voice a firm anchor in the midst of her turmoil. "Recovery is not a linear path. It's about learning from our setbacks, forgiving ourselves, and finding the strength to keep moving forward."

With every setback, Emily learned to embrace the lessons that came with it. She forged a deeper understanding of her triggers and vulnerabilities, arming herself with the knowledge needed to navigate the treacherous waters of addiction. And through it all, Daniel remained her guiding light, a beacon of hope in the darkest of moments.

Together, they celebrated each milestone, no matter how small. The first day of sobriety became a triumph, a testament to Emily's unwavering determination. With each passing day, she reclaimed fragments of her identity, piecing them together to form a new narrative—one of resilience, courage, and unwavering strength.

As the sun rose on the horizon, casting a warm glow upon their journey, Emily found solace in the knowledge that she was no longer alone in her fight. The weight of addiction began to lighten, its grip loosening with each step forward. She discovered a newfound freedom in sobriety, a freedom that allowed her to embrace life's joys with a renewed sense of wonder.

In the company of Daniel and their shared experiences, Emily blossomed. She became a beacon of inspiration for others battling their own demons, a testament to the power of resilience and the unwavering spirit that resides within the human heart.

And so, as they stood at the precipice of a new chapter in their lives, Emily and Daniel looked out into the horizon, where possibilities stretched endlessly. The scars of addiction had become a testament to their strength, a reminder of the battles they had fought and the victories they had won.

With Daniel's hand firmly clasped in hers, Emily took a deep breath, feeling the warmth of the sun on her face. In that moment, she knew that no matter what challenges lay ahead, she had the resilience to face them head-on. And together, they would continue to walk the path of recovery, a path paved with hope, courage, and the unwavering belief in the power of the human spirit.

Amidst the embrace of a supportive community, Emily found solace in the shared journey of recovery. The therapy sessions became her sanctuary, where she unraveled the tangled threads of her past and sought understanding amidst the chaos. Each word uttered in the circle of support groups echoed with empathy and shared experiences, as if the very air vibrated with healing.

As Emily sat among her fellow seekers of sobriety, she listened intently to their stories of triumph and struggle. Their voices intertwined, creating a symphony of resilience that resonated deep within her soul. In those moments, she realized that she was not alone in her battle, that there were others who had fought similar demons and emerged victorious.

Through the therapeutic process, Emily discovered the power of vulnerability. She learned to peel back the layers of her guarded heart, exposing her wounds and fears to the compassionate eyes of her peers. It was in the safety of these spaces that she realized true strength lay not in stoicism but in the willingness to ask for help, to share her burdens with others who understood the weight they carried.

As the sessions unfolded, Emily felt the walls around her heart crumble, making way for connections that ran deeper than mere surface-level interactions. She forged friendships forged in the fires of adversity, bonds woven together with threads of understanding and empathy. Together, they lifted each other up, serving as pillars of support during the darkest moments of their individual journeys.

In the hushed whispers of therapy rooms, Emily discovered the power of her own voice. She found the courage to articulate her pain, to confront the demons that had haunted her for so long. With every word uttered, she shed layers of shame and guilt, reclaiming her narrative one syllable at a time.

"I never knew the strength that lies in vulnerability," Emily shared, her voice quivering with emotion. "Opening up about my struggles and hearing the stories of others has shown me that we are all human, all imperfect. And in that imperfection, there is beauty and resilience."

Her words resonated within the sacred space, their echoes reaching every corner of the room. Her fellow seekers of sobriety nodded in agreement, their eyes filled with understanding and compassion. In their shared vulnerability, they found strength, knowing that they were not defined by their past but by the choices they made in the present.

As the therapy sessions continued, Emily dove deeper into the depths of her own psyche, unearthing buried traumas and confronting the demons that had driven her to addiction. It was a painful journey, filled with tears shed and emotions laid bare. But with each step forward, she grew stronger, her resilience fortified by the knowledge that she was no longer a captive to her past.

Armed with the tools and insights gained through therapy, Emily rebuilt her shattered identity. She discovered a newfound sense of purpose, a desire to share her story and help others navigate the treacherous waters of addiction. In the rooms of support groups, she became a beacon of hope, offering a guiding hand to those who walked the path she had once treaded.

"I want others to know that they are not alone," Emily declared, her voice filled with conviction. "We are warriors, survivors, and our stories deserve to be heard. Together, we can find the strength to rewrite our narratives and embrace a life filled with purpose and fulfillment."

Her words reverberated through the room, igniting a fire within the hearts of her fellow seekers. They knew that their journeys were far from over, that there would be hurdles and setbacks along the way. But united by their shared resilience and the power of vulnerability, they were ready to face whatever lay ahead, knowing that they had the strength to overcome.

And so, in the hallowed halls of therapy rooms and the circles of support groups, Emily discovered her purpose. She became a beacon of hope, a testament to the transformative power of resilience and the unyielding spirit of those who dare to rewrite their stories. Together, they embarked on a journey of healing, bound by the unbreakable ties of understanding and the unwavering belief in the human capacity for growth and transformation.

The process of healing unfolded like a tumultuous dance, its steps unpredictable and at times maddeningly frustrating. There were days when the cravings clawed at Emily's insides, their intensity threatening to engulf her in their fiery grip. In those moments, the battle seemed insurmountable, as if the weight of her past was an anchor tied to her very being.

But Emily was no stranger to adversity. She had faced the darkest corners of her soul, and she knew the strength that lay dormant within her. With every stumble, she found the resolve to rise again, dusting off the residue of despair and forging ahead.

In the silence of her solitude, Emily whispered words of self-encouragement, her voice a resolute declaration of defiance. "I will not let my past define me," she vowed, her determination cutting through the doubts that threatened to erode her progress. "I am stronger than the cravings that haunt me. I am more than the mistakes I've made."

Her inner dialogue became a lifeline, a constant reminder of her worth and her capacity to overcome. She visualized herself as a warrior, clad in armor forged from resilience and tenacity. Each day became a battle, fought not with swords and shields, but with unwavering willpower and a commitment to her own well-being.

Amidst the turbulent waves of temptation, Emily sought refuge in her support network. She reached out to her sponsor, whose voice became a beacon of guidance in the darkness. "You've come so far," her sponsor reminded her gently. "Remember why you started this journey, and hold onto that with all your might."

Their conversations were a lifeline, grounding Emily in moments of doubt and reminding her of the progress she had already made. They provided her with tools to navigate the treacherous terrain of triggers and cravings, teaching her the importance of self-care and the power of seeking help.

The road to recovery was not without its setbacks. There were moments when Emily stumbled, her resolve momentarily faltering. But with each setback came a renewed sense of determination, a deepening understanding of her own resilience. She learned to view relapses not as failures, but as opportunities for growth and self-reflection.

"I won't let this define me," Emily declared, her voice tinged with both frustration and determination. "I am not defined by my mistakes, but by my ability to rise again. I will learn from this and continue on my path towards healing."

As time passed, Emily discovered that her sobriety was not simply about abstaining from substances, but about creating a life rich with purpose and meaning. She pursued new passions and rediscovered old ones, finding solace in art, music, and the beauty of the natural world.

In the serene embrace of a sunlit garden, Emily marveled at the delicate petals of a blooming flower. Its resilience, she realized, mirrored her own journey. "We both rise from the darkness," she whispered, a smile tugging at the corners of her lips. "We both find beauty in the process of healing."

The road to recovery was a winding one, filled with both triumph and tribulation. Emily knew that her battle was not over, that there would be challenges yet to come. But armed with the knowledge that she was stronger than her past, she walked forward with unwavering determination.

As the sun dipped below the horizon, casting its golden hues across the sky, Emily's footsteps echoed with purpose. She was no longer defined by her addiction or the mistakes of her past. She was a survivor, a warrior of resilience, and she would continue to write her own story, one chapter at a time.

As the embers of her own healing continued to glow, Emily's passion for helping others ignited like a wildfire. She felt a calling deep within her soul, a responsibility to share her story and extend a hand to those who still wandered through the shadows.

With each word she spoke, Emily's voice carried the weight of her own experiences and the empathy forged through her own battles. She stood before crowds, her eyes brimming with compassion, as she shared the intimate details of her journey. Her words, like a gentle breeze, swept through the hearts of those who listened, whispering tales of redemption and the power of resilience.

In the dimly lit auditorium, the audience leaned forward, captivated by the raw vulnerability in Emily's voice. She painted vivid pictures with her words, invoking the depths of despair she had once known and the light she had found in the darkest corners of her being.

"There is strength in vulnerability," Emily spoke, her voice carrying a quiet strength that commanded attention. "We are not defined by our struggles, but by our capacity to rise above them. Each one of us has a story to tell, and in sharing our stories, we find solace, connection, and hope."

Her words resonated, their impact rippling through the room. Faces softened, tears glistened, and hearts opened as Emily's authenticity kindled a flame within each listener. She reminded them that they were not alone, that their battles were not in vain, and that there was a light waiting to be discovered on the other side of darkness.

In the wake of her powerful speeches, Emily received messages of gratitude and solidarity from individuals whose lives she had touched. Strangers became allies, united by the common thread of resilience. They reached out, sharing their own stories, seeking guidance, and finding solace in the understanding of someone who had walked a similar path.

Emily's advocacy extended beyond the stage. She poured her energy into grassroots initiatives, partnering with local organizations to raise awareness, provide resources, and break down the stigma surrounding addiction and mental health. Together, they created spaces of healing, where individuals could find support, guidance, and a sense of belonging.

The walls of Emily's office were adorned with colorful posters and handwritten notes, each a testament to the lives she had touched. She listened to the stories of those who sought her counsel, offering guidance with a gentle touch and a compassionate ear. "You are not alone," she whispered, her voice a lifeline for those drowning in their own despair. "You are stronger than you realize, and I believe in you."

Through her advocacy, Emily discovered a profound sense of fulfillment. She witnessed the transformative power of hope as individuals reclaimed their lives, stepping into the light of their own resilience. Their journeys mirrored her own, a testament to the indomitable spirit that resides within each of us.

The world took notice of Emily's unwavering commitment to making a difference. Media outlets sought her voice, eager to amplify her message of resilience and inspire others to seek help. Her name graced magazine covers and television screens, her image a symbol of hope for those yearning for a second chance.

But amidst the accolades and recognition, Emily remained grounded. She understood that the true measure of her impact was not in the spotlight, but in the lives she touched. Her purpose was not to be a figurehead, but a companion on the journey of healing, guiding others toward their own paths of recovery.

As the years passed, Emily's advocacy work continued to flourish. She expanded her reach, sharing her story on international platforms and connecting with individuals from all walks of life. Her words became a beacon of hope in the darkest corners of the world, shining a light on the power of resilience and the possibility of redemption.

Emily's journey was a testament to the human spirit, a reminder that from the depths of despair, seeds of hope could blossom. She had risen from the ashes of her own addiction, not only reclaiming her life but dedicating it to helping others find their own path to healing. With every step she took, Emily left an indelible mark on the world, reminding us all that there is strength in vulnerability, and that resilience can turn even the harshest of battles into stories of triumph.

In the depths of her darkest moments, as the weight of addiction threatened to crush her spirit, Emily's indomitable will began to stir. She stood at the precipice of a decision, her heart heavy with the memories of her past but determined to carve a new future.

The night air was crisp as Emily ventured into the moonlit wilderness, the moon casting an ethereal glow upon her determined face. The whispers of the wind carried the echoes of her pain, but within those whispers, she heard the faintest murmurs of hope.

"I will not let this define me," Emily whispered to herself, her voice resolute and unwavering. "I am more than the scars that mark my skin. I am a survivor."

With each step she took, the ground beneath her seemed to tremble with anticipation, as if nature itself sensed the magnitude of her resolve. The path ahead was shrouded in uncertainty, but Emily was no longer afraid of the unknown. She had tasted the bitterness of despair and now craved the sweetness of redemption.

As she ventured deeper into the wilderness, a symphony of life unfolded around her. The rustle of leaves whispered encouragement, and the distant call of a night owl seemed to cheer her on. The moon bathed the landscape in a silvery glow, illuminating the path before her as if guiding her towards a newfound destiny.

In the solitude of the night, Emily's mind danced with memories of her past. She could still feel the weight of addiction, the clutches of despair that had threatened to consume her. But amidst the pain, she found solace in the flicker of resilience burning within her.

"I am not defined by my past," she declared, her voice echoing through the stillness. "I am defined by the strength I possess in this very moment, and the choices I make moving forward."

As Emily walked, the scars on her skin seemed to shimmer with a newfound significance. They were no longer marks of shame but symbols of triumph, etchings of resilience that told a story of survival. Each step she took was a testament to her determination, leaving imprints on the earth that whispered tales of a woman who refused to be broken.

The night grew colder, and the journey became more treacherous. But Emily's spirit burned like a beacon, guiding her through the darkness. With every challenge she overcame, her resilience grew stronger, and her purpose became clearer.

In the silence of the night, as the stars shimmered above, Emily found herself standing on the edge of a precipice—a precipice that symbolized not only her personal journey but also the countless lives she would touch with her story of triumph over adversity.

"I will not be silenced," she vowed, her voice resounding with an unwavering determination. "I will use my scars as a testament to the resilience of the human spirit. I will inspire others to find their own strength and rewrite their stories."

With those words, Emily raised her head, her eyes shimmering with a newfound sense of purpose. The weight of her past no longer burdened her; it fueled her. She had emerged from the depths of addiction, a phoenix rising from the ashes, ready to illuminate the path for others still lost in the shadows.

And so, with a heart filled with hope and a spirit unyielding, Emily embarked on a journey not only to reclaim her own life but to become a guiding light for others in their own quest for redemption.

# Chapter 3: Unexpected Allies

With newfound sobriety coursing through her veins, Emily embarked on a quest that would redefine her existence. The bustling city streets became her canvas, and she moved through them with a newfound purpose and determination. The buildings rose like monuments of possibility, their windows shimmering with the hopes and dreams of countless souls.

As Emily wandered through the labyrinthine streets, she couldn't help but notice the stark contrast between the bright lights that adorned the main thoroughfares and the hidden pockets of darkness that lay in the forgotten alleyways. It was in these shadows that she discovered the untold stories, the lost souls yearning for redemption.

Her steps echoed through the narrow passages, the sound blending with the distant hum of city life. Her eyes scanned the graffiti-covered walls, each vibrant stroke of paint representing a whispered cry for understanding. Amidst the chaos, she found solace in the art that adorned the city, the intricate murals that spoke of resilience, unity, and hope.

And then, like a serendipitous encounter, Emily's gaze met the eyes of a young artist, his hands stained with the colors of his craft. He stood before a wall covered in vivid strokes, pouring his heart and soul into the creation before him. There was an instant connection, an unspoken understanding that transcended words.

"Your art is breathtaking," Emily said, her voice filled with genuine admiration. "It captures the raw emotions that lie within us all."

The artist turned, his eyes widening with surprise. "Thank you," he replied, a hint of vulnerability in his voice. "I believe art has the power to heal, to connect us to our deepest truths."

They stood there, two souls brought together by circumstance, their shared experiences pulsating through the air. In that moment, Emily realized that even in the darkest corners of the city, there were glimmers of light waiting to be discovered.

Together, they wandered through the city, seeking out the hidden gems that lay off the beaten path. In small cafes tucked away in quiet corners, they found kindred spirits who had also emerged from the depths of addiction, each one weaving their own tapestry of resilience and redemption.

The city became a tapestry of interconnected lives, each thread representing a story of triumph over adversity. Emily listened to the stories of the people she encountered, their voices filled with vulnerability and strength. They shared their struggles, their victories, and the lessons they had learned along the way.

With each encounter, Emily's own understanding of resilience deepened. She realized that it wasn't just her own story that mattered, but the collective stories of all those who had fought against the tides of darkness. They were a testament to the power of the human spirit, to the capacity for transformation and growth.

As the city lights illuminated the night sky, Emily couldn't help but feel a sense of wonder. The city, with all its complexities and contradictions, had become her ally in the journey of rebuilding her life. It had become a stage for her to showcase the power of resilience, to inspire others to embrace their own journey of redemption.

And so, with a heart brimming with gratitude and a soul fueled by the strength of her own resilience, Emily continued her quest, navigating the city's labyrinthine streets with a newfound sense of purpose. Along the way, she would encounter more unexpected allies, each one adding a brushstroke to her own tapestry of healing and hope.

One evening, as the support group meeting began, Emily's eyes were immediately drawn to a woman named Grace. Grace sat with an air of quiet confidence, her posture exuding a sense of inner strength. Her eyes, like windows to a hidden world, shimmered with a mix of resilience and compassion.

Intrigued by Grace's aura, Emily found herself inching closer, yearning to know more about this enigmatic woman. As the meeting progressed, Grace shared her own harrowing journey, her voice carrying a weight that commanded attention. Her words resonated with every person in the room, offering a glimpse into a life shaped by adversity and triumph.

After the meeting, Emily mustered the courage to approach Grace. She spoke with a mixture of awe and vulnerability, her voice laced with a longing for connection. "Your story touched my soul," Emily admitted. "I feel like we share a similar strength, a resilience born out of hardship. Can we talk further? I would love to learn from you."

Grace's eyes softened with understanding, and a small smile graced her lips. "I sensed a kindred spirit in you," she replied, her voice gentle yet filled with wisdom. "Sometimes, the people we meet on our journeys are sent to us for a reason. Let's find a quiet corner where we can share our stories and offer support to one another."

They found a secluded corner in the meeting room, the walls bearing witness to countless tales of survival. Emily and Grace settled into their seats, their eyes locked in an unspoken pact of mutual understanding. As they began to share, the room seemed to fade away, leaving only their voices weaving through the air.

Emily listened intently as Grace unraveled her life's tapestry, the trials and triumphs intertwining to form a narrative of resilience and transformation. Her words painted vivid images of strength, vulnerability, and the power of embracing one's own journey. The room filled with a palpable energy, as if the walls themselves were infused with the essence of their stories.

Touched by Grace's candor, Emily opened up about her own struggles, the battles fought, and the moments of triumph that had shaped her into the person she had become. They traded stories like precious gifts, offering support and understanding in a way that only kindred spirits can.

As their conversation drew to a close, a profound sense of gratitude washed over Emily. She knew that meeting Grace was no mere coincidence. Grace had become more than just a mentor; she had become a guiding light, a source of inspiration on Emily's path to healing and self-discovery.

With a warm embrace and a promise to stay connected, Emily bid farewell to Grace, their hearts forever intertwined. As she stepped back into the world, she carried Grace's wisdom like a beacon, knowing that her encounter with this extraordinary woman had forever changed the course of her own journey.

In the days that followed, Emily would often reflect on the words shared, drawing strength from the memories of their meeting. Grace had reminded her that resilience was not merely surviving, but thriving in the face of adversity. And armed with this newfound understanding, Emily continued on her quest, ready to face whatever challenges lay ahead, knowing that she had a kindred spirit by her side, even if only in spirit.

Their friendship blossomed gradually, like a fragile flower pushing through hardened soil. Grace became Emily's steadfast confidante, a beacon of unwavering support and guidance in a world that often felt overwhelming. Their connection grew through shared moments of vulnerability and understanding, their conversations a delicate dance of trust and empathy.

As the sun set on a tranquil evening, Emily and Grace found themselves nestled in a cozy corner of a quaint café. The soft glow of candlelight flickered against their faces, casting shadows that mirrored the intricate layers of their intertwined stories. The air hummed with anticipation, as if the universe itself recognized the significance of their bond.

Grace's voice, laced with both strength and tenderness, filled the space between them. "Our journeys have been marked by scars," she said, her eyes reflecting the memories etched deep within her soul. "But it is through these scars that we find the strength to heal and grow. They remind us of the battles we've fought and the victories we've won."

Emily leaned in, captivated by the ebb and flow of Grace's words. "How did you find the resilience to overcome your own demons?" she asked, her voice a whisper that held a touch of awe.

Grace's gaze met Emily's, the weight of her experiences mingling with a sense of hope. "Resilience," she replied, her voice tinged with wisdom, "is often born from the depths of our darkest moments. It is not a constant state, but rather a flame that flickers within us, guiding us forward even in the face of adversity."

Emily's eyes shimmered with gratitude, recognizing the profound truth in Grace's words. It was in this tender exchange, amidst the gentle murmur of the café, that she understood the significance of their friendship. Grace had become more than a confidante; she had become a guardian angel, guiding Emily toward her own reservoir of resilience.

Their conversations continued to unravel the intricate tapestries of their lives. Grace shared stories of resilience and transformation, her words painting vivid images of triumph and the power of embracing one's truth. Emily, in turn, opened her heart wide, revealing the depths of her struggles and the fragments of resilience she had discovered along her own journey.

With each passing day, Emily found herself standing taller, fortified by the strength she drew from Grace's unwavering presence. The scars that marked their paths became symbols of survival, etchings of resilience that transformed into beacons of hope.

Their friendship became a sanctuary, a sacred space where vulnerability was celebrated, and healing was nurtured. In their shared experiences, they found solace, comforted by the knowledge that they were not alone in their battles.

As they parted ways that evening, Emily felt a renewed sense of purpose coursing through her veins. Grace had gifted her the courage to face the world head-on, to embrace her own journey, scars and all. With the echoes of their conversations lingering in her heart, Emily stepped out into the world, ready to continue her own quest for resilience, guided by the light of Grace's unwavering friendship.

Their bond, forged through the fires of adversity, would forever serve as a reminder that even in the darkest moments, there is always a flicker of hope. And as Emily walked into the night, the stars above seemed to shine a little brighter, illuminating the path she was destined to follow.

Together, Emily and Grace embarked on thrilling adventures that seemed inconceivable in their darkest days. They navigated the labyrinthine streets of the city, their footsteps echoing with the rhythm of newfound freedom. Each corner turned revealed a hidden gem, a secret haven waiting to be explored.

One day, they found themselves wandering through a vibrant market, the air alive with the aroma of exotic spices and the symphony of voices haggling for treasures. Emily's eyes widened with wonder as she took in the kaleidoscope of colors and the tapestry of cultures converging in this bustling hub.

Grace grinned, her eyes sparkling with mischief. "Ready for an adventure?" she asked, a mischievous glint in her eye.

Emily nodded eagerly, a sense of anticipation bubbling within her. They weaved through the crowd, their laughter mingling with the melodic notes of street musicians. They sampled flavors from far-flung corners of the world, savoring the sweet and spicy sensations that danced on their tongues.

As dusk settled over the city, Emily and Grace found themselves in a tranquil park, a hidden oasis amidst the chaos. The scent of blooming flowers filled the air, their colors vibrant against the backdrop of a setting sun. They settled on a park bench, their eyes drawn to the sky as stars began to sprinkle the velvet canvas.

Emily leaned back, her voice filled with awe. "I never imagined that life could be so beautiful," she whispered, her words carried away by a gentle breeze.

Grace's smile held a touch of contentment. "Sometimes, the beauty lies in the moments we never thought possible. In the midst of darkness, we find the strength to embrace the light."

Their laughter carried on the wind, a symphony of joy and resilience intertwining. In each other's company, they discovered the power of friendship, the transformative energy that arises when two souls come together in pursuit of healing and adventure.

Their escapades became more than mere moments of leisure; they became a testament to their resilience and their determination to embrace life to its fullest. They soared above their pasts, embracing the present with open hearts and wide smiles.

In the embrace of nature's tranquility and the warmth of their friendship, Emily and Grace found solace. They discovered that even amidst the chaos of the world, there were moments of serenity waiting to be found, moments that reminded them of the strength they carried within.

As they watched the stars twinkle above, Emily and Grace realized that their journey was not just about surviving but about thriving. Together, they vowed to continue their adventures, to create new memories, and to celebrate the beauty that could be found in even the simplest of moments.

And as the moon rose high above them, casting a gentle glow upon their intertwined hands, Emily and Grace knew that their friendship was a gift— one that had the power to heal, to uplift, and to remind them that no matter how dark the night, there would always be a glimmer of light to guide their way.

Through Grace's gentle encouragement, Emily discovered her talent for writing. It was within the sanctuary of her thoughts that Emily's words came alive, dancing across the pages of her journal like delicate brushstrokes on a canvas. The ink-stained parchment became a portal to a realm where she could weave tales of resilience, hope, and the raw vulnerability of the human spirit.

One evening, as the sun dipped below the horizon, casting a warm glow over Emily's writing nook, she found herself sharing her latest creation with Grace. The words tumbled from her lips, each syllable carrying the weight of her experiences and the longing to reach out to others.

Grace listened intently, her eyes locked on Emily's face. When the last word escaped into the quiet room, a hushed silence hung in the air. Then, Grace's smile bloomed, radiating warmth and pride.

"Emily, your words have a power that can change lives," Grace whispered, her voice filled with awe. "You have a gift for bringing emotions to life, for painting pictures with your words. Your stories have the potential to heal hearts and ignite flames of hope in those who read them."

Emily's heart swelled with gratitude, her eyes misting with tears. To know that her words had the ability to touch others, to offer solace and inspiration, was a realization that stirred her soul.

"I want to use my words to create a ripple of change, to remind others that they are not alone," Emily murmured, her voice brimming with determination. "Through my stories, I want to give voice to the silenced, to kindle the fire of resilience within every reader."

Grace's eyes gleamed with a mixture of pride and anticipation. "You have a profound purpose, Emily. Your words have the potential to transcend barriers and ignite a spark of hope in the hearts of those who need it most."

With Grace's unwavering support and Emily's newfound conviction, they embarked on a collaborative journey, blending Emily's powerful stories with Grace's expertise in publishing and advocacy. Together, they crafted a book that would become a beacon of light, a roadmap for others seeking solace and strength in the face of adversity.

In the quiet hours of the night, as the city slumbered and the stars illuminated the sky, Emily poured her heart onto the pages, her pen gliding across the paper as if guided by an unseen force. With each sentence, she bared her soul, intertwining her own triumphs and tribulations with characters who mirrored the struggles of countless individuals.

Days turned into weeks, and weeks into months, as Emily and Grace meticulously shaped their creation. The manuscript became a tapestry of emotions, interwoven with threads of resilience, hope, and the power of second chances.

When the final words were penned, a profound sense of accomplishment settled within Emily's being. She knew that her stories had the potential to touch lives, to offer a lifeline to those drowning in their own battles.

With anticipation and a flicker of nerves, they submitted their manuscript to publishers, hoping that their words would find their way into the hands of those who needed them most. And as they awaited the verdict, Emily's heart swelled with a mixture of excitement and trepidation, knowing that regardless of the outcome, she had already achieved a victory—she had found her voice and used it to inspire others on their own journeys of resilience and self-discovery.

As Emily's writing gained recognition, the literary world buzzed with whispers of her talent. Her words had found their way into the hands of readers who were captivated by the raw honesty and profound emotions they evoked. Among those touched by her stories was Michael, a distinguished editor known for his discerning eye and knack for discovering literary gems.

One crisp autumn morning, as the leaves painted the city streets with hues of gold and amber, Emily received a letter that would change the course of her journey. Unfolding the parchment delicately, her heart quickened as she read Michael's words, written with an unmistakable air of admiration and belief in her potential.

"Emily," the letter began, "your words have the power to ignite a flame within the hearts of readers. Your stories possess a raw honesty and an unyielding spirit that resonates deeply. I believe you have a rare gift, a voice that deserves to be heard by the world."

Emily's hands trembled as excitement and nervousness intertwined. Michael's offer presented an opportunity to amplify her message, to reach an even wider audience with her stories of resilience and hope. It was a chance to illuminate the paths of those who felt trapped in the labyrinth of their own circumstances.

With a determined glint in her eyes, Emily dialed Michael's number, her voice steady but laced with anticipation.

"Michael, I'm honored by your belief in my words," she began, her voice carrying a mixture of gratitude and determination. "To know that my stories have touched you and others, to have the chance to give voice to those who have been silenced, it's a privilege I don't take lightly."

Michael's voice, warm and resonant, filled the airwaves. "Emily, your stories are a beacon of hope. They have the power to inspire, to create empathy, and to remind us all of the resilience that resides within us. I want to be a part of this journey, to help bring your words to the world."

The weight of the moment settled over Emily, both exhilarating and humbling. She had dreamed of this opportunity, but now it lay before her, the realization of her aspirations. With a steadying breath, she responded, "Michael, I'm ready to share my story, to lend my voice to those who are yearning to be heard. Together, let's illuminate the darkness and offer a lifeline of hope."

And so, Emily and Michael embarked on a collaborative dance of words and revisions, their passion fueling the creative process. Each draft was a step closer to unveiling the heart-wrenching beauty of Emily's stories, meticulously crafted to inspire, to heal, and to ignite a flicker of hope in the depths of readers' souls.

Days bled into nights as the manuscript underwent its transformation, words rearranged and polished to perfection. Emily's vulnerability spilled across the pages, merging with Michael's expert guidance and editorial finesse. The result was a literary masterpiece that shimmered with authenticity and resonated with the trials and triumphs of the human spirit.

When the final edits were made, a sense of accomplishment mingled with nervous anticipation. Emily's heart beat with a mixture of gratitude and excitement as the manuscript made its way into the hands of the publishing house's decision-makers. She knew that regardless of the outcome, her words had already carved a path of impact and connection.

And as Emily awaited the verdict, she whispered to herself, "No matter what happens, I've already won. My stories have found a home within the hearts of those who needed them most, and I will continue to write, to inspire, and to give hope to those who have yet to find their voice."

Little did she know that her journey had only just begun. The path ahead would be illuminated by the light of her words, leading her to places she had never imagined, and touching the lives of countless individuals yearning for the solace and inspiration her stories provided.

With trepidation and excitement intertwining, Emily sat at the sleek wooden desk, surrounded by towering shelves filled with literary treasures. The room seemed to hold its breath as she signed the publishing deal, the weight of the pen in her hand a tangible reminder of the magnitude of this moment. She knew that her words, like ink spilled upon parchment, had the power to transcend the boundaries of time and space, to touch hearts and change lives.

As her book, adorned with an exquisite cover that mirrored the depth of its contents, made its way into the hands of eager readers, an avalanche of emotions surged through Emily's being. She sat in her cozy study, sunlight filtering through the window, illuminating the dust particles dancing in the air. With each passing day, messages poured in, arriving in the form of heartfelt letters, tear-stained emails, and social media posts that echoed with gratitude.

"I wept as I turned the pages of your book," wrote one reader, their words drenched in vulnerability. "Your courage to share your own struggles gave me the strength to confront my own demons. Thank you for reminding me that I am not alone."

Another reader, a single mother, sent a handwritten note that spoke of resilience and hope. "Your words spoke directly to my weary heart," she penned. "In your story, I found solace and a renewed sense of purpose. You have shown me that even amidst the darkest of storms, there is always a flicker of light waiting to guide us home."

Each message became a beacon of affirmation, affirming the power of Emily's vulnerability, the impact of her story. The letters and messages became her companions, cherished tokens that reminded her of the lives she had touched and the change she had ignited.

As the words of praise multiplied, Emily's voice gained strength. Invitations poured in for speaking engagements, book signings, and interviews. She stood before packed auditoriums, her voice steady, her gaze unwavering, as she shared her journey, offering a lifeline of hope to those who hung onto her every word.

In the midst of this whirlwind, Emily never lost sight of the responsibility that came with her newfound platform. She remained grounded, her humility a constant companion. "It is not just my story," she would often say, her voice carrying a blend of gratitude and purpose. "It is the collective story of all those who have found strength in vulnerability, who have risen from the ashes of their own struggles."

Through the pages of her book, Emily had woven a tapestry of resilience, compassion, and the indomitable nature of the human spirit. Her words echoed in the hearts of readers, providing solace to the broken, a spark to the lost, and a gentle reminder that no matter the depths of darkness, there is always a glimmer of light waiting to be discovered.

And as she sat in her study, the air alive with the scent of possibility, Emily whispered to herself, "This is only the beginning. There are still stories to be told, hearts to be touched, and lives to be changed. I will continue to write, to share my truth, and to remind the world that even in the face of adversity, we can find strength, hope, and the beauty of our own resilience."

Emily's newfound purpose propelled her beyond the confines of the city, like a bird freed from its cage, soaring across vast horizons. With a map spread before her, she traced the winding paths that would take her from town to town, from bustling metropolises to sleepy villages, in a quest to ignite hope and kindle the flames of resilience in hearts hungry for inspiration.

As Emily embarked on her book tour, she found herself standing before audiences eager to hear her words. The venues varied, each with its own unique ambiance—a grand theater with velvet-draped seats, a cozy bookstore with shelves stacked high, or a sunlit community center buzzing with anticipation. The air crackled with electricity, a symphony of whispered conversations and shuffling feet.

With each step she took onto the stage, Emily felt a surge of energy, the weight of expectation and possibility. The spotlight bathed her in its warm glow, casting long shadows behind her as she began to speak. Her voice, clear and resonant, weaved a symphony of emotions, conjuring images that danced in the minds of her listeners.

In each city she visited, Emily encountered individuals whose lives had been touched by her words, their faces etched with stories of triumph and resilience. They approached her with open hearts, sharing their own journeys, their voices blending seamlessly with hers. Conversations flowed like rivers, carrying tales of struggle, redemption, and the unbreakable human spirit.

"I read your book in one sitting," a woman confessed, her eyes shimmering with tears. "Your story gave me the strength to face my own battles. Thank you for reminding me that I am not alone."

A young man approached, his voice filled with gratitude. "Your words helped me find my voice," he said, his hands trembling. "I thought I was alone in my struggles, but your story made me realize that there is a community of survivors, of warriors who refuse to be defined by their scars."

With each encounter, Emily felt her own spirit renewed, fueled by the resilience she saw reflected in the eyes of those who had journeyed alongside her. The tapestry of humanity unfolded before her, its threads intricately woven, connecting strangers through shared pain, shared strength.

In the quiet moments between events, Emily would often find herself gazing out of hotel windows, her thoughts drifting to the countless souls she had met along the way. The landscapes transformed as she traveled—rolling hills gave way to bustling cityscapes, and small-town squares brimmed with stories waiting to be shared. And in every place she visited, she left a trace of hope, a whisper of courage, an imprint of resilience that would linger long after her departure.

As the book tour drew to a close, Emily stood on a hilltop, the horizon ablaze with the hues of a setting sun. Her heart swelled with gratitude for the journey she had embarked upon—the connections forged, the lives touched, the stories shared. The world felt both vast and intimate, a tapestry of humanity with its joys and sorrows, its triumphs and tribulations.

And as Emily watched the sun dip below the horizon, she whispered, "This is only the beginning. There are still hearts to mend, dreams to ignite, and stories yet untold. I will continue to travel, to listen, and to share the power of resilience. For in each shared story lies the potential to heal, to inspire, and to weave the threads of humanity into a tapestry that embraces us all."

But it was in the most unexpected encounter that Emily found a sense of home she had long yearned for. In a small coastal town nestled between rugged cliffs and the endless expanse of the sea, she met Benjamin, a man whose eyes mirrored the depths of the ocean—calm yet teeming with unspoken stories. Their paths converged like a meeting of fate, as if the universe had conspired to bring their wounded souls together.

On a windswept beach, with the salty air caressing their faces and the crash of waves as their symphony, Emily and Benjamin shared their vulnerabilities, their triumphs, and their scars. Their conversations flowed effortlessly, like water tracing intricate patterns in the sand, weaving tales of resilience and hope. They spoke of the storms they had weathered, the lessons learned, and the unwavering spirit that refused to be extinguished.

"I never thought I would find someone who truly understands," Emily whispered, her voice carried by the ocean breeze. "But here you are, a beacon of light amidst the darkness."

Benjamin smiled, his eyes shimmering with a mixture of pain and tenderness. "We are two souls who have danced with shadows," he said. "But in each other's presence, we find solace, a refuge from the storms that once threatened to engulf us."

As they walked along the shoreline, their footsteps leaving imprints in the sand, Emily felt a sense of belonging she had long yearned for. Benjamin's presence anchored her, his touch mending the cracks in her fragile heart.

Together, they navigated the intricacies of their shared pasts, weaving a tapestry of understanding and acceptance.

In the quiet moments, they would sit on weathered driftwood, gazing out at the endless expanse of the sea, its vastness mirroring the infinite possibilities of their newfound connection. The horizon stretched before them, an invitation to dream, to heal, and to build a future together.

"I believe that our scars tell a story," Benjamin murmured, his voice carrying the weight of wisdom. "They are not symbols of brokenness but reminders of our resilience. We have the power to rewrite our narrative, to create a love that transcends the boundaries of pain."

And as the sun dipped below the horizon, casting a golden glow over the horizon, Emily and Benjamin found solace in each other's arms. They had traveled different paths, weathered different storms, but in that moment, they realized they were no longer defined by their pasts. They were two souls who had found shelter in each other, forging a home in the sanctuary of their shared love.

In the gentle embrace of the coastal breeze, as the waves whispered tales of healing, Emily knew that her journey of resilience had led her to the place she had always longed for—a place where scars were worn with pride, where brokenness birthed strength, and where the power of love could mend even the most shattered of hearts.

With Benjamin by her side, Emily continued to navigate the intricate dance of life, their steps harmonizing in perfect rhythm. In their shared sanctuary, nestled amidst the rolling hills of the countryside, love blossomed like wildflowers, painting their world in vibrant hues.

As they strolled through sun-drenched meadows, hand in hand, the scent of blooming flowers enveloped them, a fragrant symphony of nature's blessings. The wind whispered secrets of serenity, carrying their laughter and whispered promises across the landscape.

"This place," Benjamin mused, his voice laced with wonder, "it feels like home."

Emily leaned against him, her heart beating in sync with the cadence of his words. "Yes, a home we've built together, a sanctuary where our souls find solace."

In the golden hours of twilight, they sought refuge beneath a sprawling oak tree, its branches reaching towards the heavens as if embracing their love. The dappled sunlight painted their faces with warmth and tenderness as they shared dreams, aspirations, and their deepest fears.

"Life has its challenges," Benjamin confessed, his eyes reflecting the constellations above. "But together, we can face them with unwavering strength and unyielding love."

Emily nodded, her eyes shimmering with gratitude. "In your arms, I've found a safe haven, a place where my scars are understood and my dreams are nurtured."

As the moon cast its ethereal glow upon their sanctuary, they kindled a fire, its gentle flames illuminating their faces and casting dancing shadows on the canvas of their shared existence. They reveled in the quiet moments, in the hushed whispers that painted the night, reaffirming their commitment to each other.

"We are the authors of our own destiny," Benjamin declared, his voice carrying the weight of their shared journey. "Together, we can create a story of resilience, companionship, and unwavering love."

Emily leaned in, her voice a tender caress. "Let's write a tale that defies expectations, a testament to the power of love to heal and transform."

And so, in their sanctuary of love, they embarked on a new chapter of their lives, guided by the steady compass of their hearts. Through life's twists and turns, they faced triumphs and tribulations, their love serving as a steady anchor amidst the ever-changing tides.

In their sanctuary, the walls echoed with laughter, tears of joy, and whispered promises of forever. It was a place where their spirits intertwined, where the essence of their souls merged into an unbreakable bond.

With Benjamin's unwavering support and Emily's resilient spirit, they discovered that in the embrace of love, they had created a sanctuary where their hearts could flourish, where understanding and tenderness became the foundation upon which their love story was built. Together, they wove a tapestry of redemption, forging a destiny that transcended the boundaries of time and circumstance.

And as the seasons turned, their love story would continue to unfold, each chapter brimming with the infinite possibilities of their sanctuary—a place where love bloomed, resilience thrived, and their souls found everlasting solace.

With her newfound allies, Emily embarked on a transformative journey that transcended the boundaries of time and space. The path ahead unfolded like a labyrinth, its twists and turns mirroring the complexities of her own soul. Each step she took carried her deeper into the hidden recesses of her being, where profound truths lay in wait.

As Emily ventured through rugged mountain ranges and crossed turbulent rivers, nature became her steadfast companion, whispering ancient wisdom into her ear. The wind caressed her face, carrying tales of resilience from distant lands, while the earth beneath her feet seemed to echo the rhythm of her heartbeat, grounding her in the present moment.

Among towering forests, she sought solace in the embrace of majestic trees, their towering canopies offering shelter and wisdom. In their silent presence, she learned the beauty of patience and the strength that can be found in stillness.

One evening, as the setting sun painted the sky in hues of fiery gold, Emily gathered around a campfire with her allies, their faces illuminated by dancing flames. The crackling fire seemed to mirror the burning determination in their hearts as they shared stories of their own journeys.

Amidst laughter and tears, Emily's voice rose above the flickering embers. "This journey has taught me that resilience is not a solitary endeavor. It is in the connection and support of kindred spirits that we find the strength to overcome our deepest fears."

Her allies nodded in understanding, their eyes reflecting the shared wisdom they had acquired along their own paths. In the depths of their gaze, Emily glimpsed the reflection of her own growth, her once-timid spirit now standing tall and resolute.

As they continued their odyssey, traversing deserts that tested their endurance and traversing forests that challenged their perceptions, Emily's introspection deepened. The veil of illusion was lifted, and she discovered that the true power of resilience lay not in conquering the external world, but in confronting the shadows within.

In moments of solitude, she engaged in a dialogue with her own soul, unravelling the layers that had shrouded her true essence. It was a sacred communion, where vulnerability became a catalyst for transformation and self-acceptance. Through tears and whispers, she embraced the broken pieces of her past, weaving them into the tapestry of her present.

"I am more than the sum of my scars," Emily declared, her voice resonating with a newfound conviction. "My resilience lies not in erasing the wounds but in embracing them as an integral part of who I am."

With each revelation, Emily's spirit soared higher, unburdened by the weight of her past. She emerged from the depths of her own soul, a beacon of light for others who sought the path of self-discovery and resilience.

And so, with her newfound allies by her side, Emily continued her journey, her footsteps guided by an unwavering spirit. As she moved forward, the landscapes transformed, reflecting the inner transformation she had undergone. And with each step, she embraced the profound truth that resilience, like a dormant seed waiting to bloom, resided within the depths of every human soul, ready to blossom when nurtured with love, acceptance, and unwavering determination.

Driven by an insatiable thirst for knowledge and understanding, Emily set off on a pilgrimage that would take her to the far corners of the Earth. Her journey became a symphony of senses as she ventured through bustling markets, the air filled with the aroma of exotic spices and the vibrant colors of fabrics that seemed to dance in the wind.

In the labyrinthine streets of Marrakech, Emily found herself enveloped in a tapestry of sounds. The melodic calls to prayer echoed through the narrow alleyways, mingling with the laughter of children playing in hidden courtyards. With each step, the city unveiled its secrets, ancient tales whispered through the intricate patterns of mosaic tiles and the cool touch of the stone walls.

In Kyoto, Emily discovered a serene oasis of tranquility. The air was infused with the delicate fragrance of cherry blossoms, a gentle reminder of the fleeting nature of life. She wandered through Zen gardens, where meticulously raked gravel mirrored the serenity of her own mind. In the hallowed halls of temples, she immersed herself in the teachings of wise monks, their words like poetry, resonating deep within her soul.

Amidst the grandeur of ancient ruins in Rome and the ethereal beauty of the Himalayas, Emily absorbed the collective wisdom of centuries past. She sat in silence on mountaintops, feeling the pulse of the Earth beneath her, and gazed at starlit skies that seemed to hold the secrets of the universe.

Through it all, Emily engaged in dialogue with sages and seekers, learning from their experiences and sharing her own stories of resilience. In each encounter, a mosaic of cultures emerged, the common thread being the human quest for meaning and the unwavering spirit that transcends borders.

"These journeys have taught me that resilience is not bound by geography or language," Emily reflected, her voice infused with a profound sense of wonder. "It is the universal language of the human spirit, spoken in whispers of hope and etched into the tapestry of our collective existence."

As she ventured into the unknown, Emily's perception of the world expanded. The borders of her own limitations faded, replaced by a deep appreciation for the interconnectedness of all beings. With each experience, her understanding of resilience deepened, and she realized that the true essence of this quality lay not in conquering the external world, but in cultivating compassion, empathy, and a willingness to embrace the unknown.

And so, armed with the knowledge and wisdom she had acquired, Emily continued her pilgrimage, her footsteps carrying her towards new horizons and uncharted territories. With each destination, she peeled back another layer of her own being, her journey of self-discovery intertwined with the exploration of the world.

For in the vast tapestry of cultures and teachings she encountered, Emily discovered that resilience was not a destination but a lifelong pursuit, a dance between embracing the beauty of the present moment and the courage to transcend the limitations of the past. And as she moved forward, the world illuminated her path, its treasures unfolding like a story waiting to be written, inviting her to leave her own indelible mark upon its pages.

In the hushed embrace of a meditation retreat, Emily found solace from the cacophony of the world. Surrounded by towering mountains and pristine lakes, she immersed herself in the stillness of the present moment. The air carried the scent of pine and the songs of birds, weaving a symphony that resonated with the rhythm of her own breath.

In the heart of the retreat, a sanctuary of silence, Emily sat cross-legged, her eyes closed, her body grounded. Within the confines of her mind, she journeyed through the labyrinthine corridors of her past, exploring the hidden chambers of her soul. Memories, long buried and fragmented, resurfaced like ethereal whispers, beckoning her to face them head-on.

With each breath, Emily dove deeper, navigating the ebb and flow of her emotions. Tears mingled with smiles, as joy intertwined with grief, and the weight of her past pressed upon her like a heavy cloak. But she persisted, for she knew that the only way to heal was to confront the darkness within and allow the light of awareness to permeate every corner.

In the dimly lit corners of her mind, she encountered the ghosts of her past, the specters of pain and trauma that had long held her captive. They manifested as fragmented memories, half-forgotten fragments that held the power to both wound and liberate. As she stared into their eyes, she whispered, "I see you. I acknowledge your presence."

In the sacred space of her meditation, she learned to embrace these ghosts, not as adversaries, but as catalysts for transformation. With compassion as her guide, she offered them a seat at the table of her healing, inviting them to share their stories and release their grip on her soul. And as she forgave the past, she discovered a newfound freedom, a lightness that allowed her to soar beyond the confines of her pain.

"It is in the depths of our wounds that the seeds of healing are sown," Emily whispered to the universe, her voice carrying the weight of her journey. "And through the darkness, we find the courage to embrace our own light."

In the silence of the retreat, she wasn't alone. Guided by wise teachers and supported by fellow seekers on their own paths, she discovered a community united by a shared quest for healing. In whispered conversations over warm cups of tea, they exchanged stories, offering comfort and strength. Their words became a chorus of resilience, an anthem of hope that echoed through the halls of the retreat.

And as Emily emerged from the cocoon of meditation, she carried with her a newfound sense of wholeness. The fragments of her past had been woven together, creating a tapestry of resilience that adorned her soul. She walked taller, her steps imbued with a grace that came from the depths of her healing.

"I am not defined by my wounds," she declared, her voice steady and unwavering. "I am the sum of my resilience, the embodiment of my capacity to rise above the challenges that have shaped me."

And so, with her heart open and her spirit ablaze, Emily continued her journey of self-discovery. The retreat had given her the tools to navigate the currents of life with grace and compassion, and she stepped forward, ready to face whatever lay ahead, knowing that her journey of healing was infinite, and her capacity for resilience knew no bounds.

In the hallowed presence of wise gurus and spiritual mentors, Emily immersed herself in the teachings that had transcended generations. The air was filled with the scent of incense and the soft melody of chanting, creating an atmosphere that seemed to bridge the earthly realm with the divine.

As she sat in the sacred circle, surrounded by the luminous souls who had walked this path before her, Emily listened intently to the words that resonated in the depths of her being. The gurus spoke of the transformative power of forgiveness, of its ability to untangle the knots of the past and liberate the spirit.

"I carried the weight of resentment and pain for far too long," Emily confessed, her voice tinged with a mix of vulnerability and determination. "But today, I choose to release the chains that bind me. I choose forgiveness."

The gurus smiled, their eyes sparkling with the wisdom of lifetimes. "Forgiveness is not a single act, dear one," one of them said, his voice carrying the resonance of ancient wisdom. "It is a continuous journey, a choice you make every day. It is an act of compassion towards yourself and others, an offering of freedom from the burdens of the past."

Guided by their teachings, Emily embarked on a pilgrimage of forgiveness, a path that meandered through the crevices of her heart. She confronted the pain and resentment that had festered within, each step unraveling the layers of her wounded soul.

In the depths of her contemplation, she realized that forgiveness was not a pardon for the wrongs committed, but a release from the shackles of bitterness. It was an act of liberation, a choice to transcend the limitations of her own suffering and embrace the present moment with an open heart.

With each breath, Emily extended forgiveness to those who had caused her pain, and perhaps most importantly, she forgave herself. She acknowledged her own humanness, recognizing that she had carried the weight of her past with the best tools she had at the time.

In the silence of her introspection, she found the courage to let go. The burdens of resentment, anger, and hurt fell away, replaced by a sense of lightness that buoyed her spirit. With forgiveness as her compass, she set forth on a new path, one that embraced compassion and understanding.

As she stepped into the world, her heart unburdened, Emily noticed a subtle shift in her interactions with others. Compassion flowed effortlessly from her, like a gentle river washing away the remnants of judgment and resentment. She listened with empathy, her words carrying the soothing balm of forgiveness.

"I release you from the chains of my resentment," she whispered, her voice carrying the weight of liberation. "May we both find peace in this act of forgiveness."

And as Emily extended forgiveness, she also received it. The world responded with open arms, offering her the grace and acceptance she had yearned for. Relationships blossomed, bridges were mended, and a newfound sense of unity pervaded her existence.

In the embrace of forgiveness, Emily discovered the true essence of her being—a boundless reservoir of compassion and love. She understood that forgiveness was not a destination but a way of being, a journey that required daily intention and a commitment to healing.

With a heart unburdened by the weight of the past, Emily embraced the present moment with gratitude and joy. She danced through life, her steps guided by forgiveness and her spirit radiating a luminous light that touched the lives of all who crossed her path.

"I am free," she whispered to the heavens, her voice carrying the echoes of liberation. "And in my freedom, I offer the gift of forgiveness to the world."

In the sacred spaces where seekers of truth converged, Emily found a tapestry of souls yearning to unravel the mysteries of existence. There, amidst the vibrant mosaic of cultures, languages, and stories, she discovered a profound kinship that transcended boundaries.

As she sat in circles of shared wisdom, Emily weaved her words with passion, recounting the transformative power of her own journey. Her voice, like a gentle breeze, carried the essence of her experiences, captivating the hearts of those who listened.

One by one, fellow seekers stepped forward, their eyes filled with the longing for connection. They shared their own stories of triumph and tribulation, their vulnerabilities embraced by the collective understanding that pervaded the space. Tears mingled with laughter, forming a sacred elixir that nourished the souls of all.

"I, too, have known the depths of despair," a weary traveler whispered, their voice laced with raw honesty. "But in your words, I find hope. I see the reflection of my own resilience, and it ignites a fire within me."

Emily smiled, her heart swelling with gratitude. "Our journeys may differ, but the essence of our experiences unites us," she replied, her voice carrying the weight of empathy. "We are all warriors, navigating the labyrinth of life with scars that bear witness to our strength."

In these spaces of shared vulnerability, the universal language of pain and resilience became the common thread that bound them together. The wounds of the past became pathways for healing, and in their shared stories, they found solace and understanding.

As their voices intertwined, the room transformed into a symphony of compassion and collective wisdom. The air crackled with the energy of authenticity, and the walls seemed to exhale a sigh of relief, grateful for the conversations that breathed life into their silent embrace.

Emily looked around, her gaze tracing the faces of her newfound companions. They were a mosaic of diversity, each one adding a unique hue to the collective canvas of humanity. The beauty of their connection was not in spite of their differences, but because of them.

They formed an unbreakable bond, a network of souls connected by the tapestry of shared experiences. Together, they stood as living testaments to the indomitable spirit of the human journey, each story illuminating a path towards growth, resilience, and transformation.

In this sacred gathering of kindred spirits, Emily found affirmation that her journey had not been in vain. The echoes of her words reverberated in the hearts of those who listened, planting seeds of hope and inspiring others to embark on their own quests for meaning.

As the night drew to a close, the circle dissolved, but the connections forged within remained. With tearful embraces and promises to meet again, Emily and her fellow seekers dispersed, carrying the collective wisdom and resilience of their shared experiences into the vast tapestry of existence.

From that day forward, Emily knew that she would never truly walk alone. She had become part of a global community, a tapestry of humanity, where the threads of pain and resilience intertwined, reminding her that she was never truly separate from the vast web of life.

Amidst the bustling symphony of a vibrant market, Emily's eyes were drawn to a weathered face, etched with the lines of wisdom and adorned with a serene smile. She felt an irresistible pull, like a magnet drawing her closer to this enigmatic figure.

"Excuse me, sir," Emily ventured, her voice laced with curiosity. "Might you have a moment to share your wisdom?"

The old man turned towards her, his eyes sparkling with a gentle knowing. "Of course, my dear," he replied, his voice carrying the weight of years spent observing the ebb and flow of life. "What questions do you carry in your heart?"

Emily took a deep breath, her words mingling with the vibrant sounds of the market. "I seek understanding, wisdom that transcends the pages of ancient scriptures. I want to find truth in the everyday encounters, the ordinary moments that make up our lives."

The old man nodded, his gaze fixated on a distant point as he recalled his own journey. "Ah, my dear, wisdom is indeed a treasure that hides in plain sight," he mused. "In the ordinary, we find the extraordinary. Listen with an open heart, and you will hear the whispers of truth carried on the winds of everyday encounters."

Emily leaned in, captivated by his words. "But how can we recognize these moments? How can we discern the profound from the mundane?"

The old man chuckled, a sound that seemed to ripple through the bustling market, momentarily silencing the chaos around them. "The key, my dear, lies in presence," he replied. "When your senses are attuned to the present moment, the world reveals its secrets. Look beyond the surface, beyond the noise, and you will find the wisdom that has been waiting for you."

Emily nodded, absorbing the old man's words like drops of rain nourishing parched soil. "Thank you," she whispered, gratitude swelling in her heart. "I will carry your wisdom with me as I continue on my journey."

As she bid the old man farewell and merged back into the vibrant tapestry of the market, Emily felt a renewed sense of purpose. The air seemed charged with possibility, and the ordinary became extraordinary.

From that day forward, she approached each encounter as an opportunity for connection, seeking the hidden gems of wisdom nestled within everyday conversations. Whether it was the heartfelt exchange with a humble street vendor or the chance encounter with a stranger on a park bench, Emily learned to listen with an open heart, knowing that even the briefest of interactions could hold profound insights.

In these moments, time seemed to slow down, as if the universe conspired to create a space for profound connection. Ordinary words became conduits of wisdom, and strangers became messengers bearing gifts of profound truth.

Emily's journey took on a new dimension, as she sought to uncover the wisdom hidden within the fabric of existence. From the tender glances exchanged between lovers to the laughter shared among friends, she discovered that the most profound teachings were woven into the tapestry of everyday life.

In these encounters, she discovered that the world was her teacher, and the everyday moments were the pages of her own living scripture. With each interaction, her understanding deepened, and her heart expanded to embrace the boundless wisdom that surrounded her.

And so, Emily continued on her path, a seeker of wisdom in the midst of the ordinary, finding solace and illumination in the everyday encounters that breathed magic into her journey.

As the sun dipped below the horizon, casting a golden glow across the landscape, Emily stood atop a windswept hill, her gaze fixed on the endless expanse before her. A gentle breeze whispered through the tall grass, carrying with it the echoes of ancient wisdom.

"I have traveled far and wide, seeking answers and overcoming challenges," Emily murmured to herself, her voice carried by the wind. "But true resilience cannot be measured solely by external victories. It resides within, in the depths of our own being."

In the fading light, Emily felt a surge of understanding, like a flame reigniting within her. She realized that resilience was not the absence of pain, but rather the courage to face it head-on, to acknowledge the wounds and scars that life had etched upon her soul.

With each step she had taken on her journey, Emily had been sculpted by moments of both triumph and tribulation. It was in the darkest moments that her spirit had been tested, and it was through her resilience that she had found the strength to rise again.

She closed her eyes, allowing the gentle rhythm of her breath to guide her deeper into this newfound clarity. In the silence of her inner sanctuary, she embraced the duality of life—the dance between light and darkness, joy and sorrow.

"The true measure of resilience lies not in avoiding pain, but in our ability to transform it into wisdom and growth," Emily whispered, her voice carrying a profound understanding. "It is through the cracks in our hearts that the light shines brightest."

With each passing moment, the world seemed to echo her sentiments. The fading sunlight painted the sky in hues of pink and orange, a testament to the beauty that emerges from the depths of darkness.

Emily knew that her journey was not about conquering external battles, but rather about cultivating inner strength and embracing the ever-changing tapestry of life. She understood that resilience was a lifelong practice, a constant evolution of the spirit.

And so, with newfound clarity and a heart filled with gratitude, Emily continued on her path, ready to embrace the joys and sorrows that lay ahead. In the depths of her being, she carried the knowledge that true resilience was not just a destination but a way of being—an unwavering commitment to rise from the depths of pain and embrace the full spectrum of human experience.

With each step she took, the world around her seemed to shimmer with possibility, as if in celebration of her resilience. And as the winds whispered through the tall grass, carrying the echoes of her journey, Emily knew that she had found her purpose—to live a life that embraced resilience, to inspire others to embrace their own journeys, and to dance with the joys and sorrows that make us truly human.

The flickering candle cast a soft glow upon the pages of Emily's journal as her pen danced across the paper, guided by the wisdom that flowed from her heart. Words poured forth, ink staining the page with the essence of her journey—a tapestry woven with vulnerability, strength, and the transformative power of resilience.

With each stroke of her pen, Emily wove together the threads of her personal experiences and the universal truths she had unearthed on her path of self-discovery. Her words became a symphony of hope, resonating with readers who sought solace within the pages of her stories.

In coffee shops and cozy nooks, individuals huddled with her books, their fingers tracing the lines as if seeking a lifeline amidst the chaos of their own lives. Through her tales of triumph and tribulation, Emily's words became a mirror that reflected the resilience that lay dormant within each soul.

"It is within the depths of our struggles that our true strength is forged," Emily's voice echoed within the minds of her readers, a soothing melody that whispered of possibility and transformation. "In embracing our vulnerability, we find the power to rise, to overcome, and to thrive."

Her stories echoed with the shared experiences of triumphs and setbacks, offering a roadmap for those navigating their own journeys of resilience.

They spoke of the beauty that emerges from the ashes of adversity, and the unwavering spirit that refuses to be extinguished.

As readers turned the pages of her books, they discovered a kinship—a profound connection to the characters that danced across the landscapes of Emily's imagination. They felt the tug of recognition, realizing that their own stories were not isolated but intertwined with the human tapestry of resilience.

In dimly lit bookstores and bustling literary events, Emily stood before her audience, her words carrying the weight of her experiences and the power to ignite transformation. "You are not alone," she proclaimed, her voice ringing with conviction. "Within the depths of your being lies a wellspring of resilience, waiting to be embraced."

Eyes glistened with tears, hearts swelled with hope, and a sense of collective strength emanated from the room. Emily's stories had become beacons of light in a world that often felt shrouded in darkness—a testament to the indomitable spirit that resided within each individual.

And so, armed with this newfound wisdom and the power of her words, Emily continued to write, to inspire, and to ignite the spark of resilience within those who found solace within her stories. Her pen danced across the page, painting portraits of triumph and awakening the resilience that lay dormant in the hearts of her readers.

Through her written tapestries of vulnerability and strength, Emily's voice resonated across borders and generations. Her stories became a timeless testament to the resilience that defines the human experience—a reminder that within each person's journey lies the power to rise, to heal, and to thrive.

As Emily's book, a treasure trove of poignant tales, traveled across continents, it found its way into the hands of readers hungry for solace and transformation. Each page turned was a journey into the depths of the human experience, where readers saw their own struggles reflected and heard echoes of their silent battles.

From bustling cityscapes to quiet countryside retreats, readers curled up with Emily's book, their fingers tracing the lines as if caressing the pulse of their own hearts. Through her stories, they discovered a roadmap, a guide through the labyrinthine paths of healing, empowerment, and rediscovery of purpose.

In a small café tucked away in Paris, a woman with tear-filled eyes closed Emily's book, her heart both heavy with recognition and lifted with hope. "It's as if she knows the pain I've carried," she whispered, her voice barely audible, as if speaking to the spirits of her past. "But she also shows me the way out, the way forward."

In a bustling metropolis halfway across the world, a weary traveler, lost in the maze of their own thoughts, found solace within the pages of Emily's book. "These stories, they speak to me," they mused, their voice tinged with wonder. "I thought I was alone in this struggle, but now I realize we are all interconnected."

Emily's words became a bridge, connecting lives that had once seemed so disparate. They wove a tapestry of shared experiences, threading together the triumphs and trials of people from different corners of the world. Readers discovered that they were not alone in their pain, nor were they alone in their capacity for resilience.

Through the power of her storytelling, Emily created a space for empathy and understanding, fostering a sense of unity in the hearts of her readers. As they shared their stories, forged connections, and embraced their own resilience, they became a collective force—a testament to the transformative power of her words.

And so, as her book continued to traverse borders and ignite hearts, Emily's stories became whispers in the wind, spreading inspiration and healing to those who yearned for a guiding light. In the quiet corners of libraries and the cozy warmth of reading nooks, readers embarked on their own journeys, fueled by the words that danced across the pages.

Emily's book was not just a collection of stories, but a catalyst for personal transformation, an invitation to embrace the resilience that resided within.

With each turned page, readers discovered that their own stories were intertwined with the tapestry of humanity—a testament to the strength, vulnerability, and unyielding spirit that united them all.

And as readers closed the final chapter, they carried the essence of Emily's words within their souls, forever changed by the stories that had touched their hearts. They walked the path of resilience, knowing that they were not alone, but part of a collective journey—a tapestry of shared experiences, connected by the power of Emily's storytelling.

In the soft glow of the setting sun, Emily sat upon a weathered wooden bench, gazing out at the tranquil expanse of the ocean. With each rhythmic crash of the waves against the shore, memories of her arduous journey flooded her mind, intertwining with the present moment.

The ocean, vast and untamed, mirrored the depths of her soul, reflecting the fragments of her past that had once seemed irreparably broken. But now, as she traced the jagged edges of her scars, she marveled at the resilience that had woven them together, creating a mosaic of strength.

"It's been a long road," Emily whispered to the wind, her voice carrying the weight of a thousand stories. "But here, in this quiet space, I finally understand that my journey was never about reaching a destination—it was about embracing the process of becoming."

As the breeze whispered through the tall grass, Emily's thoughts unfurled like delicate petals of a flower, revealing the profound lessons that had shaped her. The power of forgiveness, once elusive, now flowed through her veins, dissolving the bitterness that had held her captive for so long.

"I've learned that forgiveness is not a sign of weakness," she murmured, her eyes fixed on the distant horizon. "It is an act of liberation—a release from the shackles of the past, allowing us to embrace the fullness of the present."

In the distance, seagulls soared, their wings outstretched as if carrying Emily's newfound understanding across the endless sky. With a gentle smile playing on her lips, she continued to unravel the threads of her journey.

"The beauty of human connection," she mused, her voice filled with wonder. "It is in the moments of shared vulnerability that we find strength. It is through our stories, our struggles, and our triumphs that we come together, weaving a tapestry of compassion and understanding."

As the sun dipped below the horizon, casting a golden glow upon the world, Emily's reflection became intertwined with the vibrant hues of the twilight. She knew that her journey had come full circle, returning her to the very essence of her being—the unwavering spirit that had carried her through the darkest nights.

"I am forever grateful for the shattered fragments," she whispered, her voice carrying a hint of reverence. "For they have given me the opportunity to rebuild myself, not as a broken vessel, but as a mosaic of resilience—a testament to the transformative power of embracing our vulnerabilities."

With a heart overflowing with gratitude, Emily rose from the bench, feeling the earth beneath her feet, grounding her in the present. She walked away from that tranquil spot, carrying the lessons etched in her soul—a beacon of hope for others who sought their own path of healing and resilience.

Her journey was far from over, but with each step forward, Emily carried the wisdom she had gathered—a guiding light for those who would cross her path. And as she embraced the unknown that lay ahead, she knew that her story would continue to unfold, one page at a time, as she embraced the ever-unfolding process of becoming.

# Chapter 5: Embracing the Tapestry of Life

The air was pregnant with anticipation as Emily stood at the crossroads, the echoes of her past and the allure of the future swirling around her. The sun, casting its warm glow upon her face, seemed to beckon her forward, urging her to embrace the unknown with open arms.

As she gazed into the distance, the landscape stretched out before her like an expansive canvas, painted with the colors of possibility. The winding roads meandered through lush green fields, leading to distant horizons adorned with majestic mountains and cascading waterfalls. Each path whispered promises of adventure and growth, inviting Emily to step outside the boundaries of her comfort zone.

With a mixture of trepidation and excitement, Emily took a tentative step, feeling the earth beneath her feet, grounding her in the present moment. Her heart thrummed with anticipation, her mind swirling with questions and dreams yet to be realized.

"It's a new chapter," she whispered, her voice carried away by the breeze. "A blank page waiting to be filled with stories of courage, love, and boundless possibility."

Her gaze shifted from the paths before her to the reflection in a nearby pond. The reflection stared back at her with unwavering determination, a mirror image of her resolve to follow her true calling.

"I have journeyed through the depths of my soul and explored the landscapes of the world," she mused, her voice tinged with a sense of wonder. "And now, I stand here, ready to embrace the next chapter of my journey."

A symphony of nature surrounded her, the melodies of birdsong and the rustling of leaves whispering their encouragement. With each breath, she felt a surge of vitality, as if the very essence of the world flowed through her veins.

"I choose the path of boldness and authenticity," she declared, her voice resonating with conviction. "I will forge my own destiny, guided by the lessons of resilience and compassion that have brought me here."

As the sun began its descent, casting a warm golden hue upon the landscape, Emily took a deep breath and took that first step forward. The crossroads faded into the distance, becoming a mere memory, as she embarked on a new chapter of her life—one filled with purpose, growth, and the unwavering belief in the power of her own story.

With each step, the anticipation grew, and Emily could feel the energy of the universe conspiring in her favor. The path ahead was uncertain, but she walked with confidence, knowing that she had already conquered mountains within herself.

And as the sun dipped below the horizon, painting the sky with vibrant hues, Emily embraced the beauty of the present moment, the excitement of the journey, and the infinite possibilities that awaited her. With an unwavering spirit and a heart filled with hope, she continued her voyage into the vast unknown, ready to create a story that would inspire others to embark on their own journey of self-discovery.

As Emily stood at the precipice of her journey, her eyes glistened with the wisdom she had gained from her experiences. The echoes of her past reverberated in her mind, reminding her of the trials she had overcome and the resilience she had discovered within herself. The wind danced through her hair, carrying with it the whispers of the lessons she had learned along the way.

"In every moment," she murmured, her voice laced with a newfound understanding, "there lies a tapestry of emotions and experiences. To truly grow and find fulfillment, I must embrace the entire spectrum of life, both its brilliant hues and its darker shades."

As if in response to her declaration, the world around her seemed to come alive with vibrant colors. The flowers bloomed with unabashed vibrancy, their petals embracing the sunlight as they swayed in the gentle breeze. The birds soared overhead, their wings a symphony of movement and freedom.

Emily's gaze shifted to the horizon, where the sky transformed into a painting of swirling hues. The golden rays of the setting sun intermingled with streaks of crimson and purple, casting a breathtaking panorama across the expanse. It was a visual reminder that beauty could be found not only in the brightest of moments but also in the shadows that whispered of growth and introspection.

"Life is a tapestry," she murmured, her words carried by the wind. "And within its intricate threads lie the joys, the sorrows, the triumphs, and the challenges that shape our very existence."

As she took a step forward, her heart swelled with gratitude for the journey that had brought her to this moment. The laughter, the tears, and the moments of quiet introspection had woven together to create a rich and vibrant tapestry that she now wore with pride.

Her voice grew stronger as she continued, "I will embrace every stitch of this tapestry—the threads of resilience, the hues of connection, and the patches of forgiveness. For it is in the harmony of these contrasting elements that true growth and fulfillment reside."

As the sunlight bathed her in its warm embrace, Emily closed her eyes, allowing herself to be enveloped by the symphony of life surrounding her. She could feel the energy of the universe pulsating within her, urging her to step forward with confidence and embrace the duality of existence.

With a deep breath, she opened her eyes, her gaze set firmly on the path ahead. The world stretched out before her, an ever-unfolding canvas awaiting her touch. And as she took that first step, her spirit ablaze with determination, she knew that the journey ahead would be an exploration of both light and shadow—an exquisite dance of resilience and growth.

"I am ready," she whispered, her voice carrying a resolute tone. "Ready to embrace the tapestry of life, to weave my story within its threads, and to create a symphony of resilience and fulfillment."

And so, with every step she took, Emily vowed to honor the colors of her tapestry, painting a portrait of strength, connection, and the transformative power of embracing the full spectrum of life's experiences.

With a fire burning in her eyes and a heart brimming with compassion, Emily set out to manifest her newfound purpose in the world. The "Wings of Resilience" foundation took flight, its name a testament to the indomitable spirit that had carried her through her own battles.

In a grand ballroom adorned with elegant chandeliers and walls adorned with inspiring artwork, Emily stood before a gathering of esteemed individuals and passionate advocates. Her voice resonated with conviction as she unveiled her vision.

"We are here tonight to ignite a spark of hope," she declared, her words commanding the attention of all those present. "Through the 'Wings of Resilience' foundation, we will uplift and empower those who have faced adversity. We will be the guiding light that illuminates their path towards resilience and a brighter future."

The room erupted in applause, a chorus of support and belief in the power of collective action.

Under the banner of "Wings of Resilience," Emily orchestrated a symphony of compassion and generosity. The foundation became a harbor of solace, its doors open wide to welcome individuals who had weathered storms and emerged stronger.

At the foundation's headquarters, nestled amidst rolling hills and surrounded by lush greenery, Emily met with those seeking solace and renewal. As she listened to their stories, her empathetic gaze mirrored their pain and their determination.

"You are not alone," Emily assured them, her voice imbued with both compassion and unwavering strength. "Within each of us lies a wellspring of resilience, waiting to be tapped into. Together, we will find the wings to soar above the challenges that have held us back."

In the hallways of the foundation, laughter mingled with whispered conversations of hope. Support groups formed, creating a tapestry of shared experiences and a network of unwavering support. Mentorship programs flourished, matching individuals with kindred spirits who had journeyed along similar paths and emerged triumphant.

In the glow of candlelit evenings, fundraisers and galas breathed life into the foundation's mission. Dazzling gowns and sharp tuxedos filled the room, as guests mingled with the shared purpose of making a difference. Auctioneers raised their paddles, their voices resounding with enthusiasm and determination to support the cause. The air was electric with a sense of collective responsibility.

Through grants and scholarships, the "Wings of Resilience" foundation provided tangible support, enabling individuals to access educational opportunities, mental health resources, and the tools necessary to rebuild their lives.

One by one, lives transformed, their trajectories reshaped by the guiding light of resilience. The foundation's success stories resonated far and wide, their impact rippling across communities and inspiring others to find strength within themselves.

Emily, adorned in the emblem of the "Wings of Resilience" foundation, stood on a stage, the spotlight illuminating her radiant smile. Tears of gratitude welled in her eyes as she gazed upon a sea of faces transformed by hope.

"Together, we have created a symphony of resilience," she declared, her voice carrying a symphony of emotions. "Let our collective wings carry us higher, spreading resilience, hope, and empowerment to every corner of the world."

As the applause thundered through the auditorium, Emily knew that the foundation's journey had only just begun. The "Wings of Resilience" had taken flight, guided by a force greater than any individual—the power of unity, compassion, and the unwavering belief in the human spirit.

In the days and years to come, the "Wings of Resilience" foundation would continue to soar, empowering individuals, weaving together stories of triumph over adversity, and reminding the world that resilience knows no bounds when ignited by a shared vision and the determination to make a difference.

Within the heart of the foundation's headquarters, a bustling hive of activity, Emily stood at the center of a gathering of passionate souls. Their eyes shimmered with determination and their voices carried echoes of hope.

"We are not just building an organization," Emily said, her voice resonating with conviction. "We are building a tribe, a sanctuary where resilience flourishes and lives are transformed. Together, we will weave a tapestry of shared experiences and unwavering support, forming a powerful network of resilience."

The room buzzed with anticipation as ideas and plans were exchanged, each word a brushstroke on the canvas of their collective vision. Walls were adorned with vibrant posters bearing empowering quotes, their colors mirroring the kaleidoscope of diversity within the tribe.

In the mornings, as sunlight filtered through the windows, the tribe gathered for discussions, their voices rising and falling like a symphony of resilience. Ideas flowed like a river, each member offering their unique perspective, sharing stories of triumph and strategies for growth.

"I have seen firsthand the transformative power of collective resilience," Emily declared, her gaze sweeping across the room, meeting the eyes of each tribe member. "Together, we will empower individuals to rise above their circumstances and embrace their inner strength. We will be a beacon of hope, a testament to the resilience that lies within us all."

The tribe forged ahead, their actions speaking louder than words. Community workshops sprang to life, creating spaces where individuals could gather, share their stories, and learn from one another. The air crackled with energy as the tribe hosted conferences and symposiums, inviting renowned speakers and experts to share their wisdom, igniting sparks of inspiration in the hearts of attendees.

Amidst the flurry of activity, Emily witnessed the transformative power of the tribe's collective resilience. Individuals who had once felt alone in their struggles now found solace and encouragement within the tribe's embrace. Walls that had kept them isolated crumbled, replaced by a tapestry woven with threads of support, understanding, and shared growth.

"I never imagined that our tribe would become such a force of change," Emily mused, her voice filled with a mix of awe and gratitude. "In each interaction, we plant seeds of resilience that bloom into incredible journeys of personal transformation."

Outside the headquarters, the tribe extended its reach into the wider community, organizing events that bridged divides and brought people together. In parks and community centers, they created safe spaces for individuals to express their vulnerabilities, to celebrate their strengths, and to discover the power of collective resilience.

"This is not just our story," Emily proclaimed, her voice echoing through the gathering of tribe members. "This is a story of countless individuals who have found hope and healing within our tribe. Let us continue to uplift one another, knowing that together, we are unstoppable."

As the tribe embraced new challenges, they discovered that the strength they had cultivated within themselves was magnified by their shared purpose. With every obstacle they overcame, their bond deepened, and their collective resilience grew.

In the evenings, around a crackling bonfire, tribe members gathered, their laughter mingling with the whispers of gratitude. They shared tales of triumph and vulnerability, their voices harmonizing like a chorus of resilience.

"This tribe is a testament to the human spirit," Emily reflected, her gaze fixed on the dancing flames. "In our collective resilience, we find not only strength but also a reminder of our interconnectedness. Together, we are writing a new narrative of hope, compassion, and unwavering support."

And so, the tribe of resilience continued to grow, each member leaving an indelible mark on the tapestry they wove together. Through their shared commitment and unwavering belief in the power of collective resilience, they became a beacon of hope, lighting the way for those who needed it most.

Underneath the canopy of a serene forest, bathed in the gentle rays of the setting sun, the tribe gathered for a transformative retreat. The air was infused with a sense of serenity as individuals from different walks of life, bound by their shared pursuit of resilience, found solace within the sacred space.

"I want you to close your eyes and breathe," Emily's voice resonated, carrying a soothing cadence. "Feel the weight of your burdens lifting as you immerse yourself in this moment. Here, within the sanctuary of our retreat, you are surrounded by a tribe that understands, supports, and uplifts you."

Participants sat in a circle, their faces illuminated by the flickering glow of candlelight. In hushed whispers, they shared their vulnerabilities and deepest fears, knowing that their stories would be met with compassion and understanding.

"I have carried the weight of my past for far too long," a woman named Sophia confessed, her voice trembling. "But being here, among all of you, I feel a glimmer of hope. I see the resilience in each one of you, and it gives me strength to believe that I can overcome."

The retreat was a tapestry of healing modalities and transformative workshops. Participants immersed themselves in mindfulness practices, danced to the rhythm of their heartbeat, and shared tears and laughter in equal measure. Guided by compassionate facilitators, they dove into the depths of their emotions, shedding layers of pain and embracing the light of self-discovery.

In one workshop, a small group gathered around a table strewn with art supplies. Brushes danced across canvases as emotions took form and colors bloomed. Each stroke was an act of defiance against adversity, a visual representation of the resilience that resided within.

"This painting is a testament to my journey," Jonathan, a soft-spoken man, shared. "In the darkest moments, I found strength I never knew I had. With every stroke, I am reclaiming my story and finding my voice."

Beyond the retreats, the foundation's reach extended across continents and cultures. Workshops were organized in bustling cities and remote villages alike, offering a lifeline to individuals who had weathered their own storms.

In a vibrant marketplace in a bustling city, a group of women huddled together, their faces etched with resilience. As they shared their stories of survival, their voices intertwined, creating a tapestry of shared experiences. The market, a symphony of scents and colors, bore witness to the healing power of community.

"The Wings of Resilience foundation gave me the courage to rebuild my life," Maria, a vendor with kind eyes, shared. "Through their workshops, I discovered the strength to rise above my circumstances and provide a better future for my children."

As the foundation's influence spread, Emily traveled across continents, connecting with local communities and igniting sparks of resilience. In each new encounter, she glimpsed the transformative power of the collective, their stories intertwining to form a tapestry of shared strength.

"I've traveled far and wide, but it is in the human spirit that I find the true beauty of resilience," Emily mused, her gaze sweeping across the diverse faces gathered before her. "In each person who finds solace within our foundation, I see the reflection of my own journey. We are not alone in our struggles, and through collective resilience, we can create ripples of change that touch lives around the world."

In the embrace of the foundation's support groups, workshops, and retreats, individuals rediscovered their own strength, rewriting the narratives of their lives with threads of resilience. As the foundation's influence spread, so too did the ripple effect of empowerment and healing, echoing across continents and cultures.

In the foundation's growth and impact, Emily found fulfillment, knowing that her journey had led to something greater than herself. Through the collective resilience they nurtured, the tribe formed a tapestry of hope, weaving together the threads of transformation and reminding the world of the boundless power of the human spirit.

In the golden hues of a breathtaking sunset, Emily and Benjamin stood on the precipice of a majestic mountain, their gazes intertwined with awe and love. The wind whispered through the surrounding peaks, carrying with it a sense of infinite possibility.

"We've climbed mountains together, both literally and metaphorically," Benjamin said, his voice laced with tenderness. "Each summit we conquer is a testament to the strength of our love and the resilience we've cultivated."

Emily's eyes sparkled with a mixture of gratitude and admiration as she leaned against Benjamin's side. "These moments are a reminder that life's greatest adventures are not only found in the world's landscapes but within the embrace of a kindred spirit," she whispered, her words carrying the weight of their shared journey.

Together, they wandered through bustling markets in far-flung corners of the world, their hands entwined as they marveled at the vibrant tapestry of cultures. They sampled exotic flavors, their taste buds becoming a conduit for shared experiences and joyful discoveries.

On remote beaches, they reveled in the symphony of crashing waves and salty breezes, their footprints imprinted in the sand like a testament to their enduring love. As they strolled hand in hand along the shore, the seagulls echoed their laughter, adding a playful melody to the rhythm of their hearts.

And beneath the star-studded skies, they found solace in the quiet moments, their souls intimately connected as they gazed at the vast expanse above. The constellations became a canvas for dreams and whispered promises, as if the universe itself bore witness to their love story.

"I once thought resilience was about standing alone against the world," Emily murmured, her voice carrying a sense of wonder. "But with you,

Benjamin, I've learned that resilience is also found in the strength of our bond, the unwavering support we offer one another."

Benjamin gently brushed a strand of hair from Emily's face, his touch filled with warmth and devotion. "We are each other's sanctuary," he whispered, his eyes reflecting a deep understanding. "In the vastness of the world, we have found our home."

Together, they continued to create their own tapestry of love and adventure, their hearts intertwined like the threads of a masterpiece. As they navigated life's challenges and celebrated its joys, they knew that their resilience was not just an individual trait but a shared force that propelled them forward, hand in hand, on the grand adventure of their lives.

In the depths of a raging storm, Emily and Benjamin stood side by side, their bodies buffeted by fierce winds and raindrops that danced like shards of crystal. The tempest seemed to mirror the challenges they faced in their journey, but their love remained unwavering, a beacon of hope in the midst of chaos.

As lightning streaked across the sky, illuminating the dark clouds, Benjamin turned to Emily with a determined gaze. "We've faced countless storms together, my love," he said, his voice carrying a steadiness that defied the turmoil around them. "And in each one, we have emerged stronger than before."

Emily's eyes reflected a mix of strength and vulnerability as she clung tightly to Benjamin's hand. "These challenges test us, but they also remind us of the depth of our commitment," she replied, her words carrying a resolute conviction. "Together, we are an unstoppable force, capable of weathering any storm."

As the rain cascaded down, forming rivulets that mirrored their determination, they braced themselves against the tempest, finding solace in their shared resilience. Each trial they faced became an opportunity to strengthen their bond, to prove that love could withstand the harshest of tests.

In the aftermath of the storm, as the clouds parted to reveal a sky washed clean by rain, Emily and Benjamin stood together on a cliff overlooking the tumultuous sea. The waves crashed against the rocks below, their ferocity a testament to the challenges they had overcome.

"We are like the cliffs, my love," Benjamin whispered, his voice resonating with quiet strength. "With every crashing wave, we grow stronger, our love carving its mark into the rugged landscape of our lives."

Emily leaned into Benjamin's embrace, finding solace in the warmth of his presence. "Together, we've learned that resilience is not just about surviving the storms," she said, her voice filled with wisdom. "It's about embracing them, knowing that even amidst the chaos, our love remains unwavering."

Hand in hand, they walked away from the cliff, their steps steady and purposeful. Their journey was not without challenges, but they faced them with a shared resolve, their love becoming an anchor amidst the turbulence. With each trial they overcame, they forged a deeper connection, their bond unbreakable, their resilience an enduring testament to their love.

In the dimly lit room, Emily sat at her writing desk, her fingers gliding across the keys of her typewriter. The soft click-clack of the keys echoed through the silence as she poured her heart and soul onto the blank page. Words flowed from her fingertips like a cascade of stars, painting vivid portraits of the human experience.

Her stories were windows into the depths of the human soul, each page a portal into a world filled with triumphs and tragedies. With each book she penned, she breathed life into characters who danced off the pages and into the hearts of readers around the globe.

In a small café across the world, a young woman named Lily held Emily's book close to her heart. Tears welled in her eyes as she turned the pages, immersing herself in the journeys of characters who mirrored her own struggles. The words resonated deep within her, touching a chord she had long thought dormant.

Moved by the profound impact of Emily's words, Lily reached out to the author, sending a heartfelt letter expressing her gratitude. The letter carried not just Lily's words but the collective voice of countless readers who found solace within the pages of Emily's books.

Days turned into weeks, and Emily's mailbox overflowed with letters from readers who shared their stories of triumph and resilience. Each letter became a thread in the tapestry of human connection, weaving together disparate lives into a tapestry of shared experiences.

One evening, as Emily opened a letter from a reader named Max, she felt a surge of emotion. Max's words painted a vivid picture of how her book had transformed his life, empowering him to face his own demons and embark on a journey of healing.

Touched by Max's vulnerability, Emily reached for her pen and wrote him a heartfelt reply. "Your words have touched me deeply," she wrote. "It is through stories like ours that we find solace and strength, realizing that we are never truly alone. Our shared experiences connect us in ways we could never imagine."

As Emily's books reached the hands of readers across continents, empathy blossomed in the hearts of strangers. They saw themselves reflected in the characters' triumphs, felt the weight of their struggles, and were reminded of the indomitable spirit that resides within every individual.

In libraries, coffee shops, and cozy reading nooks, conversations sparked among readers who had never met. They discussed the profound impact of Emily's words, sharing their own stories and forging connections that transcended time and space.

Through her storytelling, Emily became a beacon of hope, a conduit for empathy and understanding. Her words ignited conversations that crossed cultural boundaries, bridging the gaps between strangers and building bridges of empathy.

In the quiet corners of the world, where the soft rustle of pages mingled with the hushed whispers of shared stories, Emily's books continued to inspire, foster empathy, and weave a tapestry of shared experiences. Each page turned was an invitation to delve deeper into the human condition, reminding readers of the resilient spirit that resides within us all.

As the sun dipped below the horizon, casting a warm golden glow across the serene landscape, Emily found herself lost in thought. The quiet moments of reflection allowed her to delve deeper into the profound truth she had unearthed on her journey.

Surrounded by the gentle whispers of nature, Emily's mind wandered to the countless faces she had encountered along her path—the weary souls, the silent fighters, the ones who had forgotten their own strength. It was then that she realized her journey was not just about her own resilience, but a testament to the resilience of humanity.

In the hushed stillness of the evening, Emily whispered to the wind, "I have seen the flickering flame of resilience in the eyes of those who have endured unimaginable pain. I have witnessed the unwavering spirit that emerges from the depths of despair. It is within each individual, waiting to be awakened."

With a renewed sense of purpose, she pledged to ignite that dormant power within others. Through her words, actions, and the foundation she had built, Emily aimed to be the catalyst that stoked the embers of resilience in those who had forgotten their own strength.

In a crowded auditorium, she stood before an eager audience, her voice resonating with conviction. "Within each and every one of you," she proclaimed, "there lies a wellspring of resilience—a flame that can withstand the fiercest storms. It is my mission to fan that flame, to remind you of the power that resides within, waiting to be unleashed."

As she spoke, her words seemed to wrap around the hearts of her listeners, filling the room with a palpable energy. Faces transformed, eyes brightened, and a collective understanding swept through the audience. They realized that within their own stories, no matter how painful or tumultuous, lay the seeds of resilience.

In the following days and months, Emily's message reverberated through the lives of those she had touched. Through workshops, retreats, and one-on-one mentorship, she guided individuals on their own journeys of rediscovering their resilience.

In a quiet room filled with flickering candlelight, Emily sat across from Sarah, a woman who had endured years of adversity. Tears streamed down Sarah's face as she shared her fears and doubts, her voice barely a whisper. Emily listened with unwavering compassion, her presence a comforting embrace.

"Sarah," Emily said gently, "I see the strength within you. It's there, waiting to be unleashed. Together, we will find the path that leads you back to your own resilience."

Sarah's eyes met Emily's, and in that moment, a flicker of hope danced within her gaze. It was as if a dormant flame had been reignited, illuminating the darkest corners of her soul. With Emily's guidance, Sarah began to unravel the layers of pain and discover the wellspring of strength that had long been overshadowed.

Through her words, her unwavering support, and the foundation she had built, Emily embarked on a journey to awaken the resilience within others. The quiet moments of reflection had brought her to a profound realization—that by nurturing the resilience of individuals, she could contribute to the resilience of humanity as a whole.

At the summit of a majestic mountain, Emily stood with her arms outstretched, the wind gently tousling her hair. The breathtaking vista spread out before her, an expansive canvas painted with vibrant hues. In that moment, she realized that the journey of resilience was not a linear path with a definitive endpoint—it was a continuous dance with life itself.

With each step she had taken, Emily had learned to embrace the uncertainty, to find solace in the ever-changing rhythms of existence. As she looked out at the vast expanse before her, she whispered to the open sky, "Resilience is not found in the pursuit of certainty, but in the surrender to the unpredictable currents of life."

As the sun dipped below the horizon, casting a golden glow on the world below, Emily continued, "In this intricate tapestry of human experience, there are moments of joy that fill our hearts with boundless elation. There are moments of sorrow that carve valleys within us. But it is within this interplay of emotions and circumstances that we truly find ourselves."

With each word, her voice carried a depth of understanding, resonating with the reader's own journey. The reader, captivated by the beauty of her insights, yearned to delve further into the intricacies of their own existence.

In the quiet stillness of the mountaintop, Emily continued to speak, her voice carrying the weight of wisdom acquired through her own trials and triumphs. "We are not defined by our pain alone, nor are we solely measured by our successes. It is the delicate interweaving of joy and sorrow, pain and triumph, that gives rise to the full spectrum of what it means to be human."

As the reader absorbed Emily's words, they felt a stirring deep within their soul—a recognition that their own journey mirrored the dance she described. They understood that resilience was not found in escaping the challenges of life, but in embracing them fully.

With a renewed sense of purpose, Emily descended from the mountaintop, ready to embrace the ongoing dance of resilience that lay ahead. She knew that the tapestry of life would continue to unfold, presenting both joys and sorrows, but she faced it with an open heart and a steadfast belief in the strength that resided within.

As she stepped onto the path before her, the reader, inspired by Emily's words and their own inner yearning for resilience, eagerly joined her in the dance. Together, they would navigate the twists and turns, the highs and lows, knowing that within the intricate tapestry of life, they would discover the true essence of what it meant to be human.

Years had woven a tapestry of change since Emily embarked on her remarkable journey of resilience. The world around her had been transformed by the ripples of her influence, and the "Wings of Resilience" foundation had blossomed into a formidable force of compassion and strength. Its reach extended to the far corners of the globe, embracing individuals from all walks of life, as they found solace, guidance, and a renewed sense of purpose within its embrace.

As the foundation's impact expanded, Emily's words remained a source of inspiration, their power transcending the boundaries of time and space. Her books, like cherished companions, found their way into the hands of readers hungry for stories that mirrored their own triumphs and vulnerabilities. Through the pages, they journeyed alongside Emily's protagonists, their hearts pounding with anticipation, their spirits soaring with hope.

In dimly lit rooms and cozy reading nooks, readers immersed themselves in the tales that danced across the pages. Words leapt off the paper, forming vivid images in their minds—a kaleidoscope of emotions and experiences that resonated deeply. With each turn of the page, they traveled alongside characters who defied adversity, who rose from the ashes of their struggles, and who discovered the unwavering strength that lay within.

"I felt as if this story was written just for me," whispered a reader, tears glistening in their eyes. "It spoke to the depths of my soul, reminding me that resilience is not a solitary journey but a shared human experience."

In book clubs and online forums, discussions blossomed, like vibrant gardens of shared insights and personal revelations. Readers, united by the transformative power of Emily's prose, discovered newfound connections and a sense of belonging. They realized that their own stories were intertwined, woven together by the universal threads of resilience, hope, and the indomitable human spirit.

Emily, humbled by the impact her words had on others, continued to pour her heart onto the page. She crafted stories that touched the very core of human existence, knowing that within the triumphs and vulnerabilities of her characters lay the echoes of countless lives. Her pen danced across the paper, as she breathed life into each character, their struggles and triumphs becoming a beacon of hope in a world hungry for resilience.

As readers closed the final chapters of Emily's books, a profound sense of gratitude washed over them. They carried her words within them, like precious talismans, reminding them of their own capacity for resilience and the power of vulnerability. They set forth into the world, their hearts ablaze with a renewed sense of purpose, ready to embrace the challenges that lay ahead.

And so, the legacy of Emily's journey of resilience lived on—a timeless testament to the resilience of the human spirit, the power of storytelling, and the profound impact one individual could have on the lives of many. As the world continued to turn, Emily's words remained a guiding light, illuminating the path for those seeking strength, healing, and the unwavering belief in the resilience that resided within.

In the stillness of her thoughts, Emily marveled at the intricate tapestry of connections that had woven itself around her. She stood in awe of the lives she had touched, their stories etched upon her heart like a symphony of resilience. Each person she had encountered, through her writing and the tireless efforts of the "Wings of Resilience" foundation, stood as a testament to the indomitable human spirit.

In the corner of her cozy study, sunlight streamed through the window, casting a warm glow upon a wall adorned with photographs. With a tender smile, Emily traced her fingers over the images, a kaleidoscope of faces and stories. She recalled the young woman who had written her a heartfelt letter, thanking her for the book that gave her the courage to rebuild her life from the ashes of addiction. She remembered the tearful embrace with a survivor of trauma, who found solace and strength within the sanctuary created by the foundation. Their stories echoed through her mind, each a testament to the transformative power of resilience.

"They told me I would never recover," whispered a voice in Emily's memory. "But your words... your words showed me that resilience is not defined by our scars, but by our determination to rise above them."

The tapestry of connections expanded beyond borders and cultures, encompassing individuals from all walks of life. In the crowded streets of bustling cities and the serene beauty of remote villages, Emily's journey had intersected with countless others, igniting a spark of hope in the darkest of corners.

Through the corridors of time, the whispers of shared experiences grew louder. The laughter of a child who discovered their own resilience, the triumph of a survivor who dared to dream again, the whispered secrets exchanged between kindred souls—each thread a testament to the human spirit's unyielding will to persevere.

Emily's heart swelled with gratitude as she gazed upon the tapestry of connections she had helped weave. She knew that her own story was but a small fragment of the grand design, a mere thread in the rich tapestry of human existence. Together, these stories formed a vibrant tableau, painting a picture of resilience and the boundless capacity of the human spirit to overcome.

With renewed purpose, Emily whispered to the tapestry of connections, "We are all woven together, bound by the shared threads of triumph over adversity. Our stories, each unique and yet interwoven, create a symphony of resilience that resonates throughout time. Let us continue to uplift, inspire, and remind one another of the strength that lies within."

As the wind rustled through the leaves outside, a chorus of voices whispered in Emily's ear, carrying the echoes of countless lives transformed. Their tales became a symphony of resilience, resounding through the corridors of history, reminding humanity of its collective power to rise above adversity. In the quiet moments of reflection, Emily knew that the tapestry of connections would continue to grow, threading together stories of triumph and reminding the world that resilience, like the threads that held them all, was an enduring and unbreakable force.

As the years unfolded, Emily's path had not been without its share of trials and tribulations. Life, with its unpredictable twists and turns, had tested her resilience time and again. Yet, she stood tall, her spirit fortified by the wisdom she had acquired on her transformative journey. With each challenge, she had discovered that resilience was not a shield that prevented pain from seeping in, but rather a steadfast companion that helped her navigate the depths of adversity.

In the twilight hours, as the world grew quiet and shadows danced upon her walls, Emily retreated to her favorite nook—a cozy corner adorned with mementos of her journey. She ran her fingers across the worn pages of her journal, tracing the inked lines that captured her darkest moments and brightest triumphs. Her eyes fell upon a faded photograph, a snapshot frozen in time—a reminder of a trial she had faced with unwavering resolve.

Memories flooded back, the emotions still raw as she recalled the weight of doubt that had pressed upon her weary shoulders. It was in those moments of uncertainty that the tapestry she had woven came alive, its vibrant colors and intricate patterns whispering tales of strength and support. The voices of her allies and loved ones reverberated in her mind, their unwavering belief in her resilience echoing through the corridors of her soul.

"Remember, Emily," a voice whispered, gentle and reassuring. "Your tapestry is not just your own creation, but a testament to the bonds you have forged along the way. Lean on us, for we are here to hold you up when the weight feels too heavy."

She closed her eyes, immersing herself in the memories that had shaped her. She could hear the laughter of her allies, the encouragement in their voices, and the tender words of love that had guided her through the darkest nights. Each thread of the tapestry, she realized, represented a shared journey, a collective strength that had woven itself into the fabric of her life.

In the silence of the night, she spoke to the tapestry, her voice filled with gratitude and reverence. "You have carried me through the storms, held me up when I stumbled, and reminded me of the resilience that resides within. Together, we have weathered the trials of life, and together we will continue to rise."

As dawn painted the sky with hues of gold, Emily's heart embraced the tapestry of connections she had nurtured. She understood that resilience was not a solitary pursuit but a symphony of support and love. In the embrace of her allies and loved ones, she found the strength to face whatever challenges lay ahead. The tapestry that surrounded her was a testament to the power of human connection, a reminder that resilience, when shared, became an unbreakable force.

With a renewed sense of purpose, Emily embarked upon each new day, her spirit fortified by the tapestry she had woven. The challenges that awaited her were but opportunities for growth, and she knew that with her allies by her side, there was no obstacle she could not overcome. The tapestry, ever expanding, held within it the collective wisdom, love, and resilience of all those who had journeyed alongside her.

As the sun climbed higher in the sky, casting its warm embrace upon the world, Emily took a deep breath and whispered to the tapestry of connections, "Together, we are bound by the threads of resilience. Let us continue to uplift and inspire one another, for in our shared journey lies the strength to overcome, and in our shared tapestry, a reminder that we are never alone."

As the seasons changed and the winds whispered tales of resilience, Emily and Benjamin's love story unfolded like a mesmerizing cinematic masterpiece. Their relationship had been sculpted by the hands of time, weathering its own storms and emerging stronger than ever before.

In the golden hues of an autumn afternoon, Emily and Benjamin strolled hand in hand through a sun-kissed park. Leaves danced beneath their feet, mirroring the ebb and flow of their intertwined lives. The air carried a crispness that mingled with their laughter, creating a symphony of joy that resonated within their souls.

They sought solace in the sanctuary of their shared bond, a refuge where vulnerability was met with understanding and unconditional acceptance. In the quiet moments, they would sit beneath the sheltering branches of a wise old tree, their words like leaves drifting gently on the breeze.

"I am grateful for your unwavering support," Emily whispered, her voice carrying a mixture of awe and gratitude. "In your embrace, I have found the courage to face my deepest fears and the strength to rise above any obstacle."

Benjamin smiled, his eyes reflecting the depth of his love. "Our journey has taught me that love is not merely the absence of hardships, but the unwavering commitment to stand together, shoulder to shoulder, through every storm that comes our way."

Their love had become an anchor amidst the turbulent sea of life—a sanctuary where they could be their truest selves, their vulnerabilities cherished and nurtured. In the quiet corners of their shared space, they spoke of their dreams, their fears, and their hopes for the future.

"It is within the sanctuary of our love," Emily mused, "that we find the courage to explore the uncharted territories of our souls. Together, we have grown and evolved, intertwining our paths in a dance of shared growth."

Benjamin nodded, his gaze filled with the depth of understanding. "Our love is a testament to the resilience that resides within us. We have learned that true strength lies not in invulnerability but in our ability to lean on one another, to embrace both the light and the shadows that shape our journey."

In their sanctuary of love, Emily and Benjamin had become each other's pillars of support, guiding one another through the labyrinth of life. They celebrated each milestone, their laughter echoing through the walls of their shared haven. And when challenges arose, they faced them as a united front, drawing strength from their unbreakable bond.

As the sun began its descent, casting a warm glow upon their sanctuary, Emily nestled her head against Benjamin's chest, feeling the steady rhythm of his heartbeat. In that moment, she knew that their love was a force that transcended time and space—an unyielding beacon of resilience.

"Together, my love," Benjamin whispered, his voice a gentle caress. "We will navigate the storms that come our way, and emerge stronger on the other side. Our love is an anchor, a sanctuary of resilience that will guide us through the darkest nights."

With their hearts entwined and their spirits united, Emily and Benjamin stepped forward into the unknown, ready to face whatever challenges lay ahead. Their love, a sanctuary of unwavering support, would be their compass as they continued to weave the tapestry of their shared resilience.

The sun dipped below the horizon, casting a vibrant palette of crimson and gold across the canvas of the sky. Emily and Benjamin stood at the edge of the world, their fingers entwined, as if holding onto the fading light itself.

Emily's eyes traced the arc of the sunset, her heart swelling with a profound sense of gratitude. She felt the weight of the lives she had touched, the souls she had ignited with hope and resilience. Each step of her journey had woven a tapestry of connection, reaching far beyond the confines of her own existence.

A gentle breeze whispered through the air, carrying the echoes of whispered gratitude and unspoken prayers. Emily turned to Benjamin, her voice soft but filled with conviction. "Do you ever marvel at how our lives have intertwined with others? How a single act of resilience can create a ripple effect that stretches across time and space?"

Benjamin nodded, his gaze reflecting the awe that danced within Emily's eyes. "It's remarkable, isn't it? The way our choices and actions can touch the lives of strangers, leaving an indelible mark on their journey. Your resilience has become a guiding light, illuminating the path for others to find their own strength."

They stood in a moment of silent reflection, embracing the power of their shared purpose. In that quiet space, Emily could hear the whispers of gratitude from those she had inspired—strangers turned friends, whose lives had been forever changed.

"I never imagined that my journey could have such far-reaching effects," Emily murmured, her voice carrying a mixture of humility and awe. "To think that a single act of resilience can ignite a flame within another, giving them the strength to rise above their own challenges. It's humbling."

Benjamin squeezed her hand, his touch grounding her in the present moment. "Your journey has reminded us all of the resilience that resides within us. By sharing your story, you've created a space where others can find solace, inspiration, and the courage to embark on their own transformative journeys."

As the last traces of daylight faded into twilight, Emily and Benjamin remained rooted in the moment, their hearts beating in sync with the rhythm of the universe. They knew that their journey of resilience had become a catalyst for change—a testament to the interconnectedness of all souls.

"It is a gift," Emily whispered, her voice carrying a profound sense of purpose. "To know that through my journey, I have ignited sparks of resilience in the hearts of others. And as their flames burn brighter, so too does the collective strength of humanity."

Together, they gazed into the depths of the horizon, where the sun had made its final descent. In that sacred space, Emily embraced the vastness of the impact she had made—the lives touched, the resilience awakened, the tapestry of connection woven.

As darkness settled upon the world, a tapestry of stars began to emerge, twinkling with the stories of countless souls. Emily and Benjamin stood as mere threads within the cosmic fabric, knowing that their journey of resilience had become a constellation of hope for all who dared to dream.

"Our journey continues," Benjamin whispered, his voice carrying the weight of infinite possibility. "Together, we will keep igniting the flames of resilience, inspiring others to rise above their challenges and embrace the fullness of their existence."

And with that shared commitment, Emily and Benjamin turned away from the sunset and stepped forward into the night, ready to embrace the unknown, knowing that their journey of resilience would forever be intertwined with the countless lives they had touched.

The tapestry of resilience unfurled before Emily's eyes, a breathtaking masterpiece woven with the threads of countless stories. It stretched beyond the boundaries of space and time, vibrant and alive with the colors of hope and determination.

As she gazed upon the intricate patterns of the tapestry, Emily could hear the whispers of the voices it carried—a symphony of resilience echoing through the ages. Each thread represented a soul, each stitch a moment of triumph over adversity. It was a living testament to the resilience that resided within the core of humanity.

She turned to Benjamin, her voice filled with awe. "Look at this tapestry, Benjamin. It's a reflection of the strength and beauty that lies within every human spirit. It reminds us that we are all connected, that our struggles and triumphs are woven together in this grand tapestry of life."

He nodded, his eyes sparkling with a deep understanding. "It's remarkable, isn't it? This tapestry transcends borders and boundaries, cultural differences and personal histories. It speaks to the universal human experience—the capacity to overcome, to rise above, and to find strength in the face of adversity."

As they stood before the tapestry, its vibrant hues seemed to pulse with an energy that resonated with their very souls. Emily's voice trembled with emotion as she continued, "This tapestry is a mirror, reflecting back to each person who encounters it the truth that they are not alone in their struggles. It reminds them that they are part of something greater, connected to a vast network of resilience and support."

Benjamin reached out, his fingers grazing the intricate threads of the tapestry. "Within the depths of our own being, we carry the seeds of resilience. It is through embracing our struggles and finding the strength to persevere that we awaken that dormant power within us."

They stood in awe, allowing the magnitude of the tapestry to sink deep into their beings. It spoke of the triumphs and challenges faced by individuals from all walks of life, a testament to the resilience that transcended the boundaries of time and place.

Emily whispered, her voice carrying a sense of reverence. "This tapestry teaches us that our stories matter. Our struggles matter. And when we come together, weaving our threads of resilience, we create a force that can transform lives and change the world."

Benjamin placed a hand on Emily's shoulder, his voice filled with a quiet strength. "Indeed, it is through our collective resilience that we inspire one another, weaving a tapestry of hope and empowerment. Our stories become the threads that bind us together, reminding us of the strength we possess within."

They stood before the tapestry, a symbol of the beauty and power of the human spirit. In its presence, they felt a renewed sense of purpose and determination. They knew that their journey of resilience had become a part of this grand tapestry, and they vowed to continue adding their threads, inspiring others to embrace their own resilience and weave their stories into this magnificent creation.

With their hands intertwined, Emily and Benjamin stepped back, their eyes lingering on the tapestry that shimmered with the resilience of countless souls. They carried with them a deep appreciation for the interconnectedness of all beings and a commitment to nurture the resilience that lay within themselves and others.

And as they turned away from the tapestry, their hearts filled with gratitude, they walked forward, ready to embrace the challenges that lay ahead, knowing that within the depths of their own being, they carried the strength and resilience needed to overcome anything that came their way.

As Emily stood before the tapestry, the magnitude of its beauty enveloped her. Each thread glimmered in the soft, golden light, intricately woven with the stories of countless individuals. She traced the patterns with her fingertips, feeling the texture of resilience under her touch.

Her voice echoed softly in the vast chamber, filled with a sense of wonder. "This tapestry is a testament to the resilience of the human spirit, a living testament to the power of hope and courage. It reminds us that life is a tapestry of experiences—a mosaic of joys and sorrows, victories and defeats."

She stepped back, her gaze sweeping over the tapestry as if trying to capture its essence in her heart. "Within this intricate weave, I have found the true meaning of resilience. It is not simply the ability to endure but to rise above, to find strength and purpose amidst the challenges we face. It celebrates the triumph of the human spirit, woven with the threads of hope, courage, and the unwavering belief in the possibility of transformation."

The tapestry seemed to shimmer in response, as if acknowledging her words. It whispered stories of resilience and whispered dreams of what could be. It spoke of the countless individuals who had contributed their own threads to this magnificent creation—a tapestry that surpassed time and space, transcending the boundaries of individual stories to become a collective narrative of resilience.

Emily turned to face Benjamin, her eyes sparkling with a mix of determination and awe. "Our own stories are but threads in this grand tapestry, Benjamin. Our journey of resilience has connected us to something greater than ourselves. It has taught us that every experience, every triumph, and every setback has a place within the intricate design of life."

Benjamin's voice carried a sense of reverence. "And as we continue to weave our own threads, we inspire others to do the same. Our stories become beacons of light, guiding others towards their own resilience and transformation. Within this tapestry, we find connection, empathy, and the strength to face whatever comes our way."

They stood side by side, their hearts filled with gratitude for the tapestry that had brought them together and the resilience that had carried them through. They knew that their own journey would continue, their threads intertwining with those of others, each adding to the beauty and strength of the tapestry.

Emily whispered, her voice carrying a sense of purpose. "Let us continue to weave our stories with courage and authenticity. Let us celebrate the triumphs and embrace the challenges, for within this tapestry lies the essence of what it means to be human—resilient, hopeful, and capable of remarkable transformation."

As they walked away, their steps filled with a newfound sense of purpose, the tapestry shimmered behind them, a radiant testament to the resilience of the human spirit. And as its threads continued to evolve and grow, weaving together the stories of countless individuals, it carried a powerful reminder—the power of resilience resides within each and every one of us, waiting to be awakened and shared with the world.

The sky transformed into a tapestry of fiery hues as the sun bid its farewell, casting its warm embrace upon the earth. Emily stood at the edge of a cliff, overlooking the vast expanse before her. A gentle breeze tousled her hair, whispering secrets of the journey that had brought her to this moment.

With a serene smile, she turned her gaze to the tapestry that lay unfurled at her feet—a vibrant mosaic of intertwined threads that shimmered in the fading light. It was a testament to the resilience of the human spirit, each thread carrying the weight of countless stories.

As the colors of the twilight painted the sky, Emily whispered, her voice filled with a sense of reverence, "This tapestry, it holds within it the triumphs, the struggles, and the indomitable strength of the human soul. It is a living testament to the power of resilience, an eternal source of solace for those who seek it."

In the distance, a solitary figure emerged from the shadows, stepping into the glow of the dying sun. It was Benjamin, his eyes reflecting the same warmth and determination as the fading light. "Emily," he said, his voice resonating with a sense of purpose, "our journey has been a tapestry of resilience—a dance with the winds of fate and the tides of change. And as we stand here, on the precipice of a new beginning, we are reminded that the tapestry will endure, carrying the stories of countless lives."

Emily reached out, intertwining her fingers with Benjamin's, their hands forming a bridge between past and future. "Indeed, Benjamin. For as long as there are battles to be fought and hearts in need of healing, this tapestry will endure. It will be a guiding light, reminding us of our own strength and inspiring others to rise above their challenges."

As darkness descended, the stars began to sprinkle the night sky like fragments of hope. Emily's smile widened, her eyes sparkling with a renewed sense of purpose. "Let us embrace the beauty of this tapestry and continue to weave our own threads. Our stories, like constellations, will guide others through the darkness, reminding them that resilience knows no boundaries."

Benjamin's voice echoed into the night, carried by the wind. "Together, Emily, we will forge a path illuminated by the resilience of countless souls. We will be guardians of hope, torchbearers of transformation."

They stood there, silhouetted against the canvas of the universe, their hands clasped, their hearts aligned. The tapestry of resilience unfurled beneath their feet, ready to carry them forward on their next chapter, and ready to receive the threads of strength, hope, and resilience that lay within the hearts of all who dared to rise.

As the stars twinkled overhead, Emily breathed in the cool night air, her voice carrying a sense of determination. "The tapestry of resilience shall endure, Benjamin. It shall be a beacon of light, a reminder that within the human spirit lies an unyielding power. And as long as there are stories to be woven, the tapestry shall weave on."

With those words lingering in the air, they stepped into the unknown, their hearts alight with the knowledge that the tapestry would continue to bear witness to the triumphs, the sorrows, and the unbreakable resilience of humanity.

The world unfolded before Emily like a vast canvas, teeming with possibilities and unknown adventures. She took a step forward, her foot sinking into the soft earth, as if imprinting her resolve upon the very fabric of existence. Her eyes shimmered with determination, mirroring the reflection of the rising sun.

As the first rays of light bathed her face, Emily turned her gaze towards the horizon, a symphony of colors spreading across the sky. She inhaled deeply, the crisp morning air filling her lungs with a sense of anticipation. "Today," she whispered, her voice carrying a blend of excitement and serenity, "I embrace the unknown, for within it lies the tapestry of resilience."

A gentle breeze rustled the leaves, as if whispering words of encouragement. Benjamin stood beside her, his presence a steady anchor in the sea of possibilities. He looked at her with unwavering faith, his eyes reflecting the determination etched on her face. "Emily," he said, his voice resonating with a quiet strength, "you have always carried the spirit of resilience within you. It is time to let it guide us forward, weaving a legacy that will touch the lives of countless souls."

Emily nodded, a smile playing at the corners of her lips. "You're right, Benjamin. The tapestry of resilience has been my companion, my compass, and my solace. And now, it is time for me to share its embrace with others. Together, we will weave a legacy that transcends time and resonates with the beating hearts of humanity."

The world seemed to hold its breath, as if waiting for Emily's next step. She reached out her hand, intertwining her fingers with Benjamin's, their palms warm against each other. "Let us embark on this journey together," she said, her voice filled with a sense of purpose. "For within the tapestry of resilience lies hope, love, and the unwavering spirit that binds us all."

They took their first steps, the ground beneath their feet pulsating with the energy of possibility. With each stride, the tapestry unfurled, revealing a path that intertwined with the lives of those they would encounter. Their footsteps left an imprint on the world, a testament to their commitment to spread resilience and light.

As they ventured into the unknown, the tapestry billowed in the wind, its threads shimmering with a kaleidoscope of emotions. Emily turned her head, her eyes meeting Benjamin's, and a knowing smile passed between them. "Our legacy will be one of hope, love, and the unwavering belief in the human spirit," she said, her voice resolute. "As we weave the tapestry of resilience, we will leave imprints of strength on the hearts we touch."

With every step they took, the tapestry grew richer, its threads intermingling and intertwining, forming a story that spoke to the depths of the human soul. And as Emily and Benjamin embraced the challenges and victories that lay ahead, they knew that their legacy would forever be woven into the fabric of existence, a testament to the resilience that resides within the hearts of all who dare to dream.

**The End**

www.ingramcontent.com/pod-product-compliance
Lightning Source LLC
Chambersburg PA
CBHW072241260726
48657CB00024BA/593